*A WOMAN'S GUIDE TO BECOMING FINANCIALLY
SAVVY, INTENTIONALLY DEBT FREE,
AND IRRESISTIBLY ABUNDANT*

FUNDAMENTALLY FRUGAL

SARA CONKLIN

FUNDAMENTALLY FRUGAL
A Woman's Guide to Becoming Financially Savvy, Intentionally Debt Free and Irresistibly Abundant

CONKLIN, SARA, Author
FUNDAMENTALLY FRUGAL
SARA CONKLIN
FrozenPennies.com

Published by:
ELITE ONLINE PUBLISHING
63 East 11400 South
Suite #230
Sandy, UT 84070
EliteOnlinePublishing.com

ISBN: 978-1-961801-60-8 (Paperback)
ISBN: 978-1-961801-61-5 (eBook)

SEL027000
BUS050030
BUS050040

Edited by Eileen Ansel Conery

QUANTITY PURCHASES: Schools, companies, professional groups, clubs, and other organizations may qualify for special terms when ordering quantities of this title. For information, email sara@frozenpennies.com.

For more information on ways to be frugal
and manage money visit
FrozenPennies.com

DEDICATION

To Donovan:
Who thinks I'm a little weird
but also thinks I can do anything and everything
(except find France on a globe).

ACKNOWLEDGEMENTS

This book was created with a LOT of support and guidance. I could not imagine this book getting published without a small shout-out to some of my favorite supporters.

To Don:
Thank you for listening—even when you have no idea what I'm rambling about. I adore you.

To Mama:
"You and me against the world!"

To Becky:
If you can make your dream come true, so can I!

To the Blogging Besties:
Ilana, Katie, Kristen, and Jill. From YouTube ideas, thumbnails, and waves from the Northway; chats about our boys, our "Legacy," and course creations; copywriting, religion, and chats on a train; family adoptions, "Two Nice Moms," and climbing mountains in

the mornings on the other side of the world... I would be lost without each of you.

To Tracie and Carly:
The best teachers in the world.

To my 1991 brothers and sisters:
Thanks for electing me Class Treasurer—you already knew. Go Tommies!!

To my niece, Cynthia:
This entire business would not even exist without your *Year Long No Spend Challenge.*

Last, but certainly not least, to the Frozen Pennies Community:
I would be remiss if I didn't acknowledge you all for the support over the years. For reading the blog posts and the eBooks, using the spreadsheets, laughing with me on YouTube and Facebook, as well as supporting me in whatever fun adventure I want to take us on next.

You are the ones putting the FUN in FUNdamentally Frugal and I appreciate you.

FROZEN PENNIES GRATITUDE

"Sara transformed my life for the better. Because of her, my husband and I paid off $12,000 of consumer debt in months, our kids are now in sports, and we are saving for our first family vacation in years. She made me understand my dreams are possible and gave me steps to make them happen. She helped change my money mindset to break the generational baggage I have carried all my adult life. I am beyond grateful and wish I had met her years ago."

Hélène H.

"I consider myself frugal, but you give me new ideas of how to better save. You inspire me to think wisely about my purchases. Thanks for helping me and others better control spending in this expensive economy!"

Kathy

"I have found many of your ideas helpful in saving additional money each month. The frugal decision making on when to spend a little more for value mirrors my own decisions in spending money. I do enjoy your timely winter pantry stock-up ideas too. Thank you!"

Maria B.

"Great guide written so anyone can identify themselves and their habits with excellent steps to resolve money issues. Gives me hope I CAN dig out of a financial hole."

Ellen B.

"All of the information has been helpful. I had been struggling with a budget and trying to buy groceries and budget bills when I came across her information."

Francis R.

"I've been struggling with my budget for a couple of years now, but Sara's teaching style helped me get my spending under control and now I can make ends meet and save money for things we want to save money for. Thank you."

Susan

"You are the ultimate teacher.... Patient, simple and funny. I very much enjoy your videos! Very informative!!"

Jeanne

CONTENTS

INTRODUCTION

"Frugal living is not about NOT spending money but spending money where you value most."

Sara Conklin

Hello frugal friends!

If you've come here from my Frozen Pennies website or YouTube channel, then you know me. If we are just meeting now for the first time, I'm sure we will become fast friends.

Maybe you picked up this book because you might be feeling stuck and are looking for answers when it comes to managing your hard-earned money more efficiently. Maybe you're a total nerd like me and interested in all things frugal living. Whatever your reason, I'm super happy to have you here.

I've been in the content creation world since 2018 when I started blogging at Frozen Pennies. Since I started writing, my main goal was reaching women who needed a little encouragement managing their money. I was a cheerleader in high school, so being a cheerleader for women didn't feel out of the ordinary, in fact it felt natural to me.

In 2022, I went all in on YouTube finding my community outside of my blog, and it changed my life.

I found a new community of midlife women who I knew I could serve well. If you know me, you know I believe that we are all here to serve one another. This is *my* purpose in life.

Even though my focus on YouTube is midlife, the blog serves women at each stage in life. I was a young woman once and that's where I learned my biggest money lessons. This book is for any woman (although I'm not excluding anyone since there are plenty of lessons for all to learn here) at any point in her life. We are an underserved and neglected community when it comes to money topics. We deserve a voice and I'm happy to offer mine and share my experiences.

As you dive into this book, I encourage you to keep both your mind and heart open. You might not have it all figured out just yet, but by the time you reach the last page, you'll see your future in a whole new light—full of achievable possibilities.

We know that money isn't what makes us happy. Steve Jobs taught me that sometimes, all the money in the world cannot fix what's broken. Even as a billionaire, he sadly still succumbed to cancer way too young, with so much more to offer.

Money can however reduce some major stressors in life and offer stability, giving you peace of mind to fully embrace what *does* make you happy in life.

1

FROM PENNIES TO PURPOSE

THE FRUGAL ROOTS THAT ANCHOR ME

"If you are always trying to be normal,
you will never know how amazing you can be."

Maya Angelou

I almost lost our house to foreclosure.

I remember walking through the front door and seeing him sitting on the edge of the couch in shorts with no shirt, his elbows propped on his knees holding that blue legal document. I can't tell you how heartbroken, disappointed, and angry he looked. There just aren't words to describe it.

Humiliated, full of shame, and embarrassed, I thought for sure Don was going to leave because I had mismanaged his money so poorly. I thought the man I had married on that hotter-than-normal day in August of 1997 soon would be packing his bags and walking out the door.

I thought our marriage was over.

Don worked so hard at a physical job on a hot, stinky papermill every day while I was a stay-at-home mom with our two little boys. It was my responsibility to care for the daily activities of the boys, one with severe special needs. This included paying bills and running all aspects of the home. Those three people counted on me to care for them at home when my husband worked outside the home so hard for us. In that moment, I felt that I had failed them all.

I come from a long line of frugal women. My Mama, my Gram, my aunt—we are all frugal. We can sniff out a good bargain and spend pennies on our food for dinner, but I didn't know how to manage that money, and I had no idea who to turn to or how to learn.

You can save money on the things you do, find ways to cut back on your grocery budget, but if you don't know how to manage your money, you will feel stressed and overwhelmed every single day.

Lying in bed at night, unable to sleep due to worry, was a big part of my identity. It was a part of who I was (and honestly, who I still am, but for different reasons). I was ashamed of my failure to manage our finances.

Yet had I sat down and talked about this with my husband, I would have opened up, been vulnerable, and, worst of all, asked for help for something that, by his admittance, he wasn't good at either. That terrified me.

I remember money always being tight growing up, yet I never remember the power company turning off the electricity for lack of payment. What would my family say if I lost our house? Where would we live with two babies? What would our friends think?

I've had some really amazing influences in my life. Not only did these individuals teach me how to be frugal, but they also taught me who I wanted to be, as well as sometimes who I *didn't* want to be.

I firmly believe that those brought into our lives are there for the lessons—the good, the not-so-good, and the AMAZING lessons that we can learn along our journey.

The women in my life have been a true blessing. I love each one of them with all my heart.

The men have brought me so much joy, and I cannot express in words at this laptop today my gratitude and appreciation for them. Their dedication and hard work are above and beyond, and I am thankful.

WHAT GRAM TAUGHT ME ABOUT STEALING SHRIMP

I grew up in the same town as my maternal grandparents and was blessed to have them a part of my everyday life. This was such a blessing, and they were very special to me and played a crucial role in my life.

While my Gramps passed in 1995, I had my Gram in my life until she passed in 2019. She was truly my best friend, and not a day goes by when I don't think about her and miss her like crazy. Gram and I would get together every week, and we enjoyed many lunches together at TGI Fridays for the ribs (also, Gram ordered an extra meal so she could take some home to eat later in the week).

I just had to grab the tissues to write this; her memory still tugs at my heart. The three deaths in my adult life that impacted me the most were my Gram, my dad, and our sweet dog Bella, our 17-year-old black lab, who I know sits right next to God in heaven.

I adored my Gramps, but did not have as much time with him in my life as I did with Gram. He was a hard worker. He worked for a paper mill—the same mill that I worked at through college along with my husband and stepdad. Gramps worked at that paper mill for 40 years before retiring due to health issues. Gram raised three kids on one income and managed everything very well. It was because of her and my mom that I learned how to cook from scratch.

Gram was the youngest of three, spoiled, and dare I say, a little selfish. She was also cheap. My Gramps gave her everything he could. He worked hard to support his family, and he provided well. He was the love of her life, and when he passed, she was heartbroken. Gram was never the same without him.

She taught me to work hard to save money in order to do what I loved. I'm sure it was Gram who influenced my love for the ocean. My Gramps had six weeks off from work every winter, so they would head down to Florida. I remember having the privilege of going to visit them in Florida during my school vacation. I flew down to spend time with them for a week. I still think of those trips and how special it was to have that kind of time with both of them.

I learned that taking vacations with them was so much fun. As a child, they took me along on some pretty cool adventures—not only to Florida but also to Nashville, Tennessee; Kings Dominion in Ohio; Canada; Maine; and many other beautiful places, too numerous to list. They took two trips across the country during their lifetime, one in a camper and one by car. As a family, we've done as much traveling as we could on a tight budget through the years. Now that we are older and in a better financial place, we plan on squeezing in as much travel as we can. I've been bit by the travel bug and if it were up to me, I would sell everything, live out of a van, and see every corner of the continent.

My grandparents bought a new house in a brand-new housing development in 1965 when housing developments were unique. They were a one-car family, and (almost) always had a new car. Their adventures were all funded by one salary, good money management, and *cheap* living at a time when the economy was weak.

It was Gram who taught me that you should always ask for a discount. I cannot remember a time in my adult life when Gram did not ask for a senior citizen discount. Her cheap nature was also borderline unethical (maybe not even borderline), and she taught me what NOT to do. I remember going to a restaurant buffet with shrimp and watching in amazement as she filled a Ziplock bag with shrimp to take back home.

She took something home from restaurants every time she ate out, mostly just sugar and jelly packets. I remember a story about when my mom was young and they went to an apple orchard to pick apples. They hid two bags of apples near the road, paid for one bag, and then picked up the other two on their way home. Yes, I am fully aware that all these things are examples of stealing, and I do not advocate that.

Even though Gram was a little selfish in many areas, I was surprised at how often she let me borrow money! When the power company turned off the electricity *again*, she would let me borrow money to pay for them to turn it back on. When our checking account was empty and our family needed food, Gram was there to bail us out with her checkbook. There were months when it was Gram who kept us fed. This was proof that as a young adult, married with a family, I was that inexperienced at managing money.

I was recently reminded that I wasn't nearly as terrible at managing money as I thought and that I really need to give my younger self some grace. I had the skills; I just needed to hone them and learn some lessons. The talent was in there. Otherwise, I would never be able to do the work I do today. This is my calling and those experiences brought me to where I was meant to be. It's true that we often learn more from our mistakes, then from getting it right the first go round.

Gram would be so proud of us if she were here right now. We are doing great, Grammy, and we miss you like crazy!

Wait... *let me grab another tissue.*

MY MAMA AND HER AWARD-WINNING PICKLES

I am proud to share that my mom's pickles have won blue ribbons at the local fair. This is one of the things about my mom that my husband loves the most—her bread and butter pickles.

My mom is a true rock star. She was a single mom for several years after my parents divorced when I just two-years-old. She married my stepfather when I was six. She worked more than one job, and I never went without. I may never have gotten everything I *wanted* but I sure had everything I *needed*. This most likely impacted my frugal approach to life in general.

I remember spending a lot of time at my grandparent's house, in addition to all the apartments in which we lived. The apartment on Bush Street might have been my favorite because we were right down the street from the beach and a lake where we could go when the weather was good. It was my favorite until the outside door at the bottom of the steps fell off and pinned my hand. However, the landlords were the nicest people. They felt just terrible and bought me ice cream after.

Mom has always had a garden and quite the green thumb. One of her favorite stories about me is from the summer of 1974 when I was just 18 months old, and she was getting me ready for a bath. She undressed me, then went into the bathroom to start the bath water, but when she returned to the living room to get me, I was *gone*. Frantically, she ran out around the house, searching every room. When she came up empty-handed, she ran out the screen door and found me naked as a jaybird sitting in the strawberry patch, eating every strawberry I could get my little hands on, regardless of the color!

She still loves to share that story.

My mom's garden was always incredible, and still is. Not only was it to help feed our family but it's always been a hobby and a passion of hers, even in her retirement years. She grows fruit, vegetables, and flowers *everywhere*. Often, she also splits up her outside flowers and propagates inside plants to share with me. Inside plants... now that is something even I can do with my brown thumb!

If you know me, you know I'm more of an inside girl. Brook, the Bug Girl (the woman who used to spray our house in the summer

7

for ants), called me Inside Sara, and she was not wrong. I love being outside by the ocean, lakes, rivers, and even the pool, but that's really the only time I like to be outside. My husband said, "If I knew the way to get you outside was to put in a pool, I would have done it YEARS AGO!"

When I was a teen and would mouth off to my mom, my punishment would be to pick beans and weed the garden. That was torture—I hated every minute of that. In fact, I'm surprised my negative energy didn't kill the entire garden.

Canning and freezing vegetables was one way she saved money on groceries. She taught me that if I wanted to save money on pickles, jams, and veggies, I should visit more often so I could return home with a box full of food, since she knows that Inside Sara does not *play* like that!

Grocery budgets were one area where my Mama flexed her frugal muscles. Paper coupons were a real thing and a big deal back in the '80s, and she perfected the technique. Everyone used them. She created a coupon box using a simple cardboard box. It was 12 inches by 18 inches and about eight inches tall. We covered the box with contact paper—brown with white, yellow, and orange flowers (probably something she picked up at a garage sale). It was organized well into categories in alphabetical order.

Every Sunday, when the paper came, we sat down together, clipped the coupons, and filed them. Then, we would match the coupons to the sales flyers so Mom could make her grocery attack plan, creating a list and a meal plan. We lived in a small town, so, we drove out-of-town for grocery trips and errands were a full-day adventure for us. We were armed with coupons and coolers.

I remember a pantry full of plain Cheerios, Raisin Bran, and oatmeal. Back in the '80s, a frugal mama could get those things for pennies with coupons, coupled with a good sale so they would stock up. I remember asking once for Lucky Charms, and Mom told me to get a job—and her reply was in that blunt, straightforward, and *slightly* rude tone of voice that I tried to convey here.

The same went for shampoo—there was no Finesse in our house. So, with the first babysitting money I earned, I bought Lucky Charms, Finesse shampoo and conditioner!

To this day, Mama shops the loss leaders and rarely buys something other than what is on sale. A loss leader is an item that the grocery store will put on the front of its sales flyer. The concept is that the store would sell the item at such a low price they would lose money on it–*all to get you into the store to spend money on other things*. Her garden in her retirement years is more incredible than ever, and I'm still going home with a bag of pickles, relish, jam, and one or two things she thought I might like from the thrift store!

Mama showed me the value of thrifting. We were pros at thrift shopping, garage sales, and church bazaars when I was growing up. We looked forward to stuffing a bag for a dollar at the Jewish Bazaar every summer. We were ROCK STARS! Even today, my mom and I plan a thrifting date at least one weekend every year. Where I live, there are no good thrift stores, but she lives on the Connecticut/Massachusetts border, which is nothing short of a gold mine and thrift stores are plentiful.

In high school, we had many events that required formal dresses: homecoming dances, speech class banquets, senior dinner dances, National Honor Society inductions, to name a few. Due to our budget limitations and our frugal nature, there was no way we would pay full price for a dress, so we bought them all second hand.

A friend from high school still talks about the olive-green dress I wore to our senior dinner dance. It was satin on top and velvet on the bottom. It was stunning and clearly from the 1950s. We also found shoes and jewelry. The shoes were a bit tight, but dang... they were perfect. So, I sacrificed comfort for fashion. I never felt deprived buying second-hand formal attire. I loved the uniqueness of our finds!

MY AUNT WITH THE AMAZING SHOES

As a child and more so as a teen, I greatly admired my Aunt Donna. I wanted to be just like her when I grew up. She was career-driven and always had finely manicured nails, fabulous shoes, and a fancy purse. In fact, Dooney & Burke was her go-to bag.

I always thought she was rich. She seemed to do well financially. She and her first husband, Uncle Bob, divorced when I was very young and she remarried again 48 years later to Uncle Tony, her long-time partner. Yes, it took them 48 years to marry. In my young mind, she had a lot of money. In hindsight, it could have been that she just had more money than we did and being frugal ran in her blood, too.

She also was very generous and took all of us on fabulous vacations, during which I learned that by saving money all year and by being frugal in other areas of life was worth doing in order to have a great vacation. Walt Disney World was a favorite vacation spot of hers and I was invited one year to ride to Walt

Disney World with my Aunt Donna and Uncle Tony, along with his three boys: Anthony, Ray, and Nick, as well as Tony's mom. It was quite a long drive in a minivan with that many people, but they rented a condo, and we all had a blast.

That was the trip on which I was introduced to Tony's three boys. I was 12, and closest in age to Anthony, who was also 12, so we became good friends.

I remember one night we were in the elevator, returning from a late fancy dinner at The Empress Lily, sadly, no longer there. While in the elevator, Anthony told me a very long joke called Rickety Rackety Stairs. It actually was a terrible joke, but one that I found hilarious. *If we ever get together for coffee, ask me to tell you. I still remember it.*

That very well might have been the moment I realized that Anthony and I had become good friends.

Later, I learned that Aunt Donna (or if you're my oldest son, Travis, she was Aunt *Dina*) also had inherited the frugal gene. Her closet was full of beautiful clothes and shoes, many designer brands, for which she never paid full price. She was a savvy, frugal shopper, just like me and my mom.

She taught me a lot about the value of work and earning money. Through her example, I learned that not only could women earn good money, women could WANT to work and earn their own money, which was nothing to be ashamed of. She taught me how to invest my earnings and grow that money from those investments.

She also taught me that it was perfectly acceptable to carry a luxury purse if you earned the money to buy it.

Aunt Donna taught me that budgeting was very simple. She said, "When you get paid, pay your bills; whatever is left is yours." As a young married mama of two boys, I remember thinking, it's not quite that simple when others rely on you to eat. It turns out that she really wasn't that far off with her budgeting principle.

ANOTHER MOTHER WITH WHOM TO SHARE BOOKS

Another one of my *frugal* mentors is my mother-in-law, Lorraine, who taught me some great lessons as an adult. One of the greatest lessons ever (and I've been known to throw it back at her a time or two) is that everyone has a choice. You can choose not to have any money, or you can choose to have three jobs. You can choose to be in your 80s and not eat (or just be super tired of cooking), or you can choose to ask for help from Meals on Wheels.

You can choose your path, discover you've taken the wrong path, and turn around to try a different path.

Lorraine and I shared a love of reading, particularly nonfiction. When she moved into a new apartment and needed to downsize, she flat-out refused to give away any of her books. As a book fanatic myself, I totally understood that. So, we found a way to maximize her space with tall bookshelves, taking up less floor space so she could keep all her beloved books.

Lorraine is a lifelong learner. She went to college later in life, graduating with her bachelor's degree at the age of 63. She earned her degree for self-satisfaction, not for her career advancement; she continued to work at JC Penney. However, she later expressed regret that she never stepped out of her comfort zone to pursue a career in her chosen field of study.

I admire that she returned later in life to further her education. College was hard at 18. Doing it in your 60s has to be three times as hard.

MY GUIDING STAR—THE NUT BURGER

I know this was the part of the book where I talked about the frugal women in my life, but it wouldn't be complete if I didn't share with you a little bit about my dad and my husband.

He was loud, obnoxious, and fun. He liked to be the center of attention, and because my Mama also liked that, there's not a question in my mind why they didn't stay married. There were other reasons, of course, but this was a big one. He called kids Nut Burgers. I never knew why but when my grandchildren do something silly, I'll pull out the goofy saying and it usually fits the context.

I'm going to need a tissue again.

He lived his life in a very simple way, by focusing solely on the ones he loved. I was never truly able to appreciate him and know him well until my adult life, but I'm forever grateful for that time before his untimely passing.

He taught me one of the most important lessons in life. We are all on this earth to serve others and that giving is a top priority. He would give you the shirt off his back in a hot New York minute if he thought you could use it more than he could—before you even asked.

Material possessions were not necessary, and a handmade gift of a gorgeous jewelry box meant more than a new 10-speed bike. You may not know it when you are 15, but you sure as heck know it at 51. Dad taught me that living a simple life based on love is far better than *any and all* material possessions.

His grandsons were the second love of his life, right after his second wife, Debbie. Two years after she passed away from cancer, he literally died of a broken heart. He had a heart attack, went in for surgery, and quickly joined her in heaven. I never got to know their true love story until later in life and that made me sad.

Dad taught me that the things others told you and your beliefs growing up (learned from your environment) are not necessarily the full truth. So, by limiting your beliefs, you are holding yourself back from the relationships you could have, as well as money you could earn.

He is a big reason why I decided to sit and write this book today: to serve others. My mission in life is to teach and help. I have the heart of a teacher, the teachings of my dad, and a life mission to help as many people as possible carefully and frugally manage their money.

A PARTNER IN CRIME

Don and I have come a long way financially from that morning when a courier hand-delivered those blue foreclosure papers to my half-asleep, outraged husband.

We started dating when I was just 20 years old. He was 33, divorced, with two kids. We lived in a small town of just 6,000 people, and I was working at the local paper mill for the summer while going to college. This was quite the scandal! A divorced 33-year-old man dating a 20-year-old young woman... the outrage! It worked for us, though and I've never looked back!

Back in the early '90s, the paper mill hired college students for the summer if the student had a parent employed there. I was what they called a *mill brat*. My grandfather had long since retired from the paper mill, but my stepdad was still employed there at that time. My (soon to be) husband was also working at the same paper mill.

We didn't meet until my second summer working there. It just wasn't our time yet. We met after his divorce—a time when we were both ready for one another. I believe it truly was kismet. We dated for five years before getting married in August 1997. Then in September 1998, we welcomed our first son, Chase. Then our second son, Donovan, arrived in April 2001.

Now married to an amazing woman with three babies, my stepson, Travis, was one of the best bonus children I could ever imagine! I've known Travis since he was four. I cannot say enough about how awesome he and his wife Krystan are. I could not be more proud of them and their precious family.

My sweet husband came to me with a lot of money baggage. As you can imagine, divorce has a way of messing with personal finances, and there was a lot of money trauma for us to work through. He also has self-diagnosed attention deficit disorder (ADD), so managing money felt impossible to him.

Hubby taught me patience and commitment—that no matter what, giving up was not an option. A funny part about Don's patience. If you ask him, he's the least patient person you would ever meet. His soul is patient, kind, and warm but he would never admit that.

Me as a child of divorce and Don as a divorcee, we agreed that marriage this time meant forever. We knew that mistakes would happen, and boy, did they ever, but we also knew that we could work through anything.

I'm unsure if I believe in the whole soulmate theory, but if I did, this might just be him.

Don stood by all through my failed business attempts, the power company shutting off the electricity more times than I can count, and almost losing our home. Most of the time, he had "angry eyebrows," but he never left my side. All children in the family know exactly what "angry eyebrows" look like and they all know to choose the next action and word carefully.

Commitment. That's what he taught me, and *love*—so much love.

Let's revisit the opening of this book quickly.

Almost losing our home to foreclosure was a pivotal moment in my financial life. I knew I had to do better. So, I went to the library, checked out every book I could get my hands on regarding money management and devised a plan. I was never going to put myself in that position again.

Luckily, the bank was able to work with us to refinance our mortgage so we could keep our home, which thankfully is the same home we live in today.

As you realize at this point, my husband did not leave. In fact, our marriage is stronger and full of more love than ever. In the process, we learned a few things about the division of labor in our home—if he was going to stick his head in the sand about the money, then he could not be mad when I messed up because while I was figuring this financial thing out, I expected I would mess up along the way. It was a bumpy ride, to say the least.

One of the books from that stack of books from the library changed my life forever and encouraged me to write my own book, which is now in your hands. This book will show you what life can look like on the other side of debt and financial struggles. I intend to be your coach and biggest cheerleader. It is my life's mission to show you what frugality looks like.

It's not about not spending money haphazardly; it's about spending with intention in the areas we value most.

I started a blog in 2018 when my niece introduced me to the concept of a spending freeze the Christmas of 2017. She challenged herself to no-spending for an entire year, and I thought, if she could do it, so could I! My son, who always knew I wanted to start a blog, piped up and said, "Mom! You should blog about it!" It was the best idea ever.

So, I started a website entitled Frozen Pennies—get it? Spending freeze, Frozen Pennies?

At first, it was just a way to journal my own no spend challenge but soon after creating the site, I felt the call to become a financial coach. Dave Ramsey offered a program for a Ramsey Solutions Financial Coach Certification. I took the course with a little bit of money that my dad left me after he passed away.

My Frozen Pennies website transformed from an online journal into a full-blown business with social media accounts, a fantastic

Pinterest account, and a phenomenal YouTube channel. Now add to all of that, this book that you are holding in your hands.

I love this work so much and cannot imagine ever doing anything different.

I started college in 1991 as a banking and finance major. Once I got to orientation, I realized I would never be able to sit in a cubicle all day in stuffy dress clothes, so I changed my major to English and planned to get my master's in secondary education. Well, I never got that master's, but I taught preschool for almost 10 years. Twenty-seven years after the orientation at State University of New York at Morrisville, all the pieces fell into place. I now write and teach all about money management.

This book is filled with tips on saving money and thoughts on mindset, retirement, debt reduction, and budgeting. It will become your one-stop-shop for finance, and you will easily be able to adapt these ideas into your own life because, personal finance is well, *personal!*

Most of all, I'm super excited to show you how much fun being frugal can actually be!

If you want some free resources to help you on your money journey, check out <u>frozenpennies.com/fun.</u>

2

FRUGALICIOUS

IT MAKES SENSE TO SAVE CENTS

"Pennies do not come from heaven.
They have to be earned here on earth."

Margaret Thatcher

Welcome to the world of frugality, where saving money is not just a habit yet a lifestyle choice that can transform your life in unexpected and joyful ways.

In a contemporary society that constantly pushes us to spend more, consume more, and want more, being frugal is like a breath of fresh air. It's about finding freedom in our choices and realizing that true happiness doesn't come from having the latest gadgets or a closet full of clothes. Instead, it's about making intentional choices that align with our values and financial goals.

Being frugal is not about not spending money. It's about spending money with intention on the things you value most.

Being frugal doesn't mean being cheap nor depriving yourself of life's pleasures. It's about being mindful and resourceful, maximizing every dollar, and finding joy in simplicity.

Frugality is a mindset that encourages us to prioritize what truly matters, whether saving for retirement, reducing debt, buying a dream beach house, or spending more time with family and friends. It's really about making room for the things that bring us genuine happiness and satisfaction.

So, why would anyone choose to be frugal? Financial security is one of the greatest gifts you can give yourself.

By adopting a frugal lifestyle, you gain control over your finances, reduce stress, and pave the way for a future filled with possibilities. You're no longer at the mercy of debt with high interest rates nor living paycheck to paycheck. Instead, you're empowered to make choices that support your long-term goals. For some, being frugal is engrained in who we are. We've learned this lifestyle from those before us and feel that there's no other way to live.

For others, it's out of necessity. The money in our bank accounts is limited, so we need to stretch it as far as we can to make ends meet. We may have unexpected expenses that come up, so we take from one pile to cover those costs, leaving a gap in our budget.

For the rest, it's a means to an end—a way to meet those goals. For them, it's not forever, it's just for now.

Frugality can offer more than just financial benefits. It can also be incredibly fun and rewarding. Imagine the thrill of finding a great deal and reducing your grocery budget by $50 for the week, the satisfaction of repurposing something old into something new, or the creativity that comes from finding cost-effective solutions for everyday problems.

Frugality invites us to slow down and appreciate the little things, turning ordinary moments into extraordinary experiences. Instead of running out to go shopping when you're bored, being frugal allows you to read, organize, and find other ways to entertain yourself.

Being frugal fosters a sense of community and connection. It encourages us to share, trade, and support one another, whether trading books or clothes with friends, organizing a neighborhood potluck, or participating in a local swap meet.

Through frugality, we learn the value of collaboration and the joy of giving, creating a richer (pun intended), more fulfilling life for ourselves and those around us.

When I asked the Frozen Pennies community what being frugal meant, 78 percent said it meant spending less overall, on quality rather than quantity, and spending with purpose. We also agreed that there is a big difference between being cheap and being frugal. They are not one and the same. We will talk more about the differences later.

A sampling of their responses include:

"Buying the best value, not always the cheapest. Frugal does not equal cheap."

"Repair instead of replace. I also have a list of things I need to do to improve my life and myself that cost nothing, so if I'm ever planning a day and have free time; I'll rifle through it and pick something."

"Best deals you can find on necessities and true happiness items. No waste, reuse, and repurpose."

Using frugality as a tool for all of the great things that it can offer you is something that I have used in my arsenal of resources to finally learn to manage money better, get out of debt, and then plan for our future. Everyone can learn to be frugal. You don't have to be born with the frugal gene to know how to use it. There are a few great frugal resources on frozenpennies.com/fun.

3

BEFORE YOU BUDGET

THE REAL REASONS WE DON'T START

"Money is only a tool. It will take you wherever you wish, but it will not replace you as the driver."

Ayn Rand

In a world in which consumerism reigns supreme, the idea of being frugal stands as a lighthouse on the coast of the financial security ocean. I know, that's super cheesy, and I'm not even going to apologize. Understanding what it truly means to be frugal goes beyond penny-pinching and dumpster diving.

I have tried EVERYTHING when it comes to budgeting, including apps, spreadsheets, binders, envelopes, sinking funds, paper planners, burying my head in the sand, throwing my hands up and screaming, "I guess I just suck at money management, and I'm just going to have to live with it!"

Sinking funds are just mini savings accounts for things that you know are coming. For example, Christmas, car repairs, and quarterly water bills all need a sinking fund. I will explain in more detail later.

I needed to keep trying because giving up definitely was not an option.

A paper planner was my magic wand to transform our financial lives. I looked at dozens online, bought a few binders, and downloaded a couple off the Etsy website, but in the end, they just weren't quite right. Something was lacking. So, I created my own. If you'd like to use it, I'm happy to share it at no cost at <u>frozenpennies.com/fun</u>.

It's the same planner I've used for years. With feedback from my community, I updated and improved it as needed. If you choose to use it, please let me know how it works for you.

Keep in mind that it doesn't matter what tool you choose to use. What does matter is that you just need a budget. My Mama always said she could keep track of everything in her head. Maybe some people are able to do that, but most of us simply cannot. Life seems a bit more complex these days as well, so maybe that's part of it. Writing down and visually processing the numbers can help us develop a plan of attack.

Quite frankly, I urge you to ditch the Apps and the spreadsheets and start with paper and an erasable pencil.

I manage money through *intentional* choices, smart budgeting, and a belief system that values quality. I'm diving into the essence of frugality, exploring the budgeting basics, and differentiating between being frugal and cheap, all while uncovering the benefits that embracing the frugal life can offer.

Here come the salty ocean metaphors.

I will be your guide on the waves of frugality, helping you navigate the waters with confidence and purpose. Join me as we dive into simplicity, intentionality, resourcefulness, and smart money management in every aspect of your midlife.

The dreaded B word is the first thing we need to discuss, my friend.

BUDGETING FOR BEGINNERS

Budgeting is a tough chore for beginners. It's scary, intimidating, and just plain hard. However, I can attest that knowing where you're spending your money, as well as how to make your dollars work better for you, will satisfy your mind, spirit, and heart.

I have heard too many reasons for not having a budget, including:

"I don't make enough money."

"I make plenty of money, so I don't need to budget."

"I'm not a math person."

"I just don't want to know."

These are all really just excuses. Knowledge really is power. You can learn skills like math. If you don't think you have enough money to create a budget, then you are the one who needs a budget the most.

If you think you don't want to know, then you have no idea what you can do. Your financial life could evolve into something AMAZING!

Even if you pay all your bills each month, set savings and investing to autopay, and have money left over for date nights and shopping sprees to your favorite stores, you are not fully aware of the potential your money *could* have for you.

WHAT HAPPENS IF YOU DON'T HAVE A BUDGET

You can call a budget whatever you want. Call it a plan, a blueprint, a money roadmap, no matter what you choose to call it, you just need something in place.

Too many of us are maxed out financially. We are anxious, stressed, and downright afraid of where we could end up tomorrow. Most of us have no idea where we will be next week or if we have enough money to last until the next paycheck. Many people believe that gone are the days of secure jobs that last decades, much less the coveted savings account for unexpected expenses.

I have been there! Gosh, have I been there?! I took the change back to the grocery store, so my husband could have money for gas. Our grocery store has a machine that you can dump loose change into and take the receipt to customer service to get your money. The machine kept eight cents out of every dollar back then, but it was still *extra* money. Mind you, I wasn't about to tell him that's what was going on. I just told him the change jar was full, and it was time. It was full because I went through everything, including purses, pockets, drawers, and cars, to collect all I could to make it to another paycheck.

Having a set budget can help with this. I can honestly say that I know now how much we have and how it is spent. When I diligently refer to my budget, much of my stress and worry disappears.

A budget has done great things for my marriage, too! There is no more fibbing and sneaking around. All items are indicated in hot pink and aqua pens for all the family to see.

BEFORE CREATING A BUDGET

One of the most crucial aspects of creating a budget is having the right mindset and attack plan. Also, remember to give yourself some grace. It takes 21 days to build a habit, but about three months of practice to create a working budget.

Understanding why it's necessary is key. Tapping into those heartfelt reasons why you might want to have more money is a valuable step. Before you even decide to create a budget, decide that you want to take control of your money.

Then, decide why you want to have control. Maybe you're tired of being stressed about money or fighting with your spouse about not having enough. Whatever the reason is, you have DECIDED that it's time.

My "why" was to never face the threat of foreclosure again, and my husband could be proud of me, not just as his wife, but as a responsible keeper of the family's money.

DISCOVER AWARENESS

When new to budgeting, it is critical to understand where you spend your hard-earned money. Financial awareness is a big eye-opener. The goal here is to spend less than you make so you can put that money towards debt and later to help build wealth or at least a financial cushion.

A budget system helps assign the correct amount to each category and indicates where you may be overspending unknowingly. Even if you don't make a lot of money, knowing where you spend it will shine a light on where you are and where you can improve.

It doesn't matter how *much* money you earn, but how you *manage* what you earn. This idea can change your life.

MAKE THE DECISION

Decide that it's time to go for it. Today is the day that you start a budget. Commit to doing this, knowing that it's not going to be perfect, and it's going to take work. Just get started. As the Nike commercial shared: *Just Do It!!*

Remember to give yourself some grace and understand that you must make changes. Sacrifices will have to happen for the greater good.

This is not forever, just for now.

4

THE BUDGET PLAYBOOK

GAME PLAN FOR SUCCESS

"It takes as much energy to wish as it does to plan."

Eleanor Roosevelt

Setting up a budget and perfecting it month after month is genuinely an art form. Let's face it, the first time anyone tries something new, it's almost guaranteed that it won't be perfect. That's okay.

I offer a free downloadable budget planner at <u>frozenpennies.com/fun</u>.

Budgeting is the hardest part for anyone. It's the most crucial and difficult step. I've found in my conversations with women over the years (and I'm sure men feel the same) that they can get to the point of setting up the budget and adding in all the numbers so every penny has a place, but the most challenging part is the follow-through. It's easy to get stuck before we begin, so we just don't start.

Remembering how a baby learns is a great correlation when implementing a budget.

I love to correlate starting a budget with a baby learning to walk. This example is probably way overused, but it works. When babies learn to walk, they will stand, try taking a few wobbly steps, and then fall. Parents and loved ones cheer them on and encourage them to try again. They don't tell the baby that they failed and should go through life crawling around the floor. That would be absurd! It takes practice to get good at anything. Even in my 50s, I'm still practicing that whole walking thing!

I did a no-spend challenge for 30 days to save my money so I could go away for a few days and write this book. While I spent time alone at the lake, I saw some super cute dogs swimming near me. As I went over to introduce myself, I twisted my ankle. The decks were multilevel, and in my excitement to meet the pups, I took a step backward, not realizing that the deck was a step down so down I went!

Luckily, the dog owner was a paramedic, looked at my ankle, and told me to ice it and rest. So, there I sat and wrote with my foot elevated for the week I was there. It took a while to heal, but I was more upset that I had to stop petting my new fur friends, Tucker and Poppy!

See, I'm still working on the *walking* thing in a literal sense.

The same concept can apply to a budget. Giving up is not an option. That is where the rubber meets the road. *The time is now, not tomorrow!* You must know where your money is going.

This step is truly eye-opening for most of my clients. Women always told me they had no idea they were spending so much on non-essentials.

TRACK YOUR EXPENSES

I still track my expenses. Through my bank's website, I physically print my monthly statement. Then, I use colored highlighters to organize my spending. Highlighting all food purchases, for example, in pink, will quickly indicate whether or not I've exceeded my food budget for the month. If so, why and how can I get back on track?

The same goes for Amazon purchases. I highlight Amazon purchases in green. I know whether I'm over budget when I see too much green.

Step 1: *Gather your financial documents.*
The first step in tracking your expenses is to gather all your financial documents. The documents include bank statements, credit card statements, receipts, bills, and any other spending records. Take time to organize these documents chronologically to clearly understand your spending habits over a specific period. I find it easiest to tackle one month at a time but make a note if some expenses come due annually or quarterly.

Step 2: *Categorize your expenses.*
Once you have all your financial documents in order, it's time to categorize your expenses. Start by creating broad categories such as your four walls (anything home related: insurance, rent/mortgage, utilities, internet, food, loan payments, and discretionary).

Discretionary spending is where all those charges are listed. Amazon, Target, Home Goods, and any place else of which you might be a victim and spend all your money.

Discretionary spending is considered anything that is non-essential. So even though you might think that Starbucks and Chick-Fil-A might fall under the food category, it's actually not essential – sorry, not sorry!! Food is essential but fast food is considered discretionary.

As you review your documents, assign each expense to its corresponding category. This step will help you identify where you're spending the most and where you may need to adjust your budget. I print my statements and use four different colored highlighters to identify spending categories, that make for a super pretty picture that swats you right upside the head.

Step 3: *Use technology to simplify the process.*
Once you complete the initial tracking, you can use budgeting apps like YNAB, Every Dollar, or Simplifi by Quicken. These apps auto-categorize your monthly spending and can save you a lot of time while giving you a clear picture of your spending.

Step 4: *Decide what you must pay and what can be cut.*
Be fierce. Be strong. . . It's time to make some cuts to free up your money. Whether to pay that looming debt or beef up that retirement plan, note how much you spend on food. That's the place that surprises a lot of people. They think they are only paying $500 for food a month when, in reality, it's a shock to see it's usually much more than that and often double what you think.

Step 5: *Review and adjust regularly.*
Tracking your expenses is not a one-time thing yet an ongoing process. Make it a habit to review your expenses regularly, preferably at the start of each month, to identify any patterns or trends that may require tweaks to your budget.

Are you consistently overspending in specific categories? Are there areas where you can cut back or find ways to save money? By staying proactive and adjusting as needed, you can stay on track toward achieving your financial goals.

UNDERSTAND MINDSET AND SHORT-TERM GOALS

Mindset and goal setting started when we explored why people may need a budget. Understanding our relationship with money will give us an open door to how to manage it and how big we can dream.

Knowing *how* you feel about money first will determine what mindset changes need to happen in order for you to embrace frugality. Mindset and goal setting are an important part of asking the question, *why do we even need a budget?* It's not *just* about tracking your dollars and cents; it's about understanding our relationship with money. This relationship shapes our behaviors, thoughts, and decisions, even though we may not even realize it. Often, these thoughts are buried deep within our subconscious and unless you are trained to hear these thoughts, they remain unheard.

By exploring how we truly feel about money, as well as recognizing the emotions that are attached, we unlock the superpower to change them. Therefore, we must replace negative or limiting beliefs with ones that empower us, we then gain the ability to shift from *just getting by* to managing our money with confidence. This allows us to dream bigger!

We all have our own money stories. How you were raised and how your parents felt about money have an impact. We are all products of our environment. Some people think money is evil, while some look at money from a place of fear and scarcity—never having enough. Others love money and, in an obsessive capacity, they can never have enough. Then there are those of us who believe money is a tool so we can not only live a life of comfort and security, but we can be generous with others and can share with children, grandchildren, parents, and whoever we want. We can give to our community: schools, libraries, firehouses, and food pantries. The more money we have, the more we can share!

The hard part comes from replacing the negative thoughts and beliefs with positive ones. Thoughts become beliefs when we repeat them over and over. Practicing positive thoughts or affirmations about money sounds super "woo" but it seriously works. Affirmations such as: money comes easily to me; I am a money magnet; money loves me; my money can change the world; and I am wealthy beyond money. These are statements I've written over and over in my journal.

You can then decide on your goals for the next three, six, nine, and 12 months, even if those goals are to stick with the budget. Knowing that this is a process and thwarting any negative talk does work. Give those super cheesy positive affirmations a try. There is something to be said about the Law of Attraction.

Do you remember the Saturday Night Live Skit with Paul Smiley? He was in the mirror talking to himself. "I'm good enough. I'm smart enough. And, gosh darn it, people like me!" Channel your Paul Smiley, but to attract financial stability.

I will address this further in the book and in fact have an entire chapter regarding positive mindset.

DEBT TRACKING AND PAYOFF

The most challenging step for a beginner budgeter is uncovering debt. Look through all the statements and bills to find account numbers and find all those account passwords online. List all debt details, including account numbers, interest rates, minimum payments, and balances.

Next, list them in order of how you want to start paying them off. I prefer the debt snowball method, which lists them from smallest to largest. Some prefer listing them from the highest to the lowest interest rate and tackling those high-interest-rate debts first. It's your choice to tackle the debt as you like, just stick with your decision.

For me, knocking out small debt first motivates me and gives me an accomplished feeling. Crossing debt off your list quickly gives you the excitement to keep going. This builds the motivation you need to get all your debt paid off. It really is an incredible feeling of freedom once the debt is paid.

Honestly, it doesn't matter. Personal finance is personal for a reason.

I'll address more on debt payoff later in the book.

INCOME AND EMERGENCY FUND

These two are the most essential parts of financial awareness and budgeting for beginners. Everyone must know how much they bring in and prepare accordingly for an emergency.

Once you really know how much money you have coming in, you will then be able to understand what to do with the amount going out. It may sound funny that some people don't know exactly how much money is coming in, but sometimes there are missed areas. Obviously, you want more money coming in than going out. For many, in it comes, out it goes. Do you need more money to meet your needs and/or wants? Are you ready to become frugal enough that incoming minus outgoing equals *doable*?

Decide that a $1,000 emergency fund and those "just in case" moments are enough for now. If you own your home, increasing it to $2,500 might make you a little more comfortable.

If we had an emergency fund back in 2005, we probably would not have gotten in over our heads. The water heater and car repairs stole our money as fast as they came in, making it seemingly impossible to pay our mortgage. Even $1,000 set aside would have been helpful.

Do whatever necessary to build an emergency fund. When we started ours, I was not only using some of our income tax returns, but we also had a garage sale, and my husband sold one of his more significant items. I was adding anything I could from our leftover grocery money, and then I moved it into an unlinked account to my checking, so it was more work for me to transfer it.

FIXED AND VARIABLE EXPENSES

Fixed expenses are those that usually remain the same every month. Budget items like rent or mortgage, cell phone, car insurance, and internet are all examples of fixed expenses. Haircuts, groceries, gas, and electric bills are all variable. They fluctuate and allow you to cut them back if needed. Variable expenses are more challenging to pin down. Looking through the past few months of bank statements will help you pull an average guestimate with which to work.

You will need to account for all these expenses and write them down.

CREATE THE BUDGET

Now that you have all the basic info you need, it's time to enter the numbers you've been collecting. However, where do you enter these numbers? You could use a notebook and pen, or some people use spreadsheets or apps.

I prefer a budget binder. I've been using this system for the past 18 years, and it's the system we credit to pay off more than $70,000 in debt, in addition to our mortgage.

Creating a zero-based budget walks you through ensuring every penny has a job. Once you pay all your bills, you will see how much money is left and decide how to allocate that.

If there isn't any money left over, then decisions will have to be made about how to make that happen. Selling things that you cannot afford is a possibility. If you have a $549 SUV payment and debt, the answer might be to sell that SUV and buy something less expensive. Even better, pay cash for a pre-owned car and eliminate a car note altogether.

The other option is to find ways to make more money. Side hustles are a real thing for many folks and increasing with the higher cost of living.

SINKING FUNDS AND CASH ENVELOPES

As a beginner budgeter, using a cash management and budgeting system is, in my professional financial coach's opinion, the best way to control your money and get out of debt.

The cash envelope's primary purpose is to force you to spend only what you have budgeted and to stop you from overspending on things you find most challenging to control, such as: groceries, clothes, dinners out, and anything that is not a true need, yet a want. A specified amount in each envelope limits your spending in those areas and stops you from exceeding the budget.

Sinking funds are mini savings accounts for things that you know are coming. Saving for Christmas, vet appointments, back-to-school expenses, birthdays—really anything you know will exceed monthly budgets. For example, try preparing a few weeks or months in advance for Christmas gifts by putting small amounts at a time in a separate savings account or in an envelope, instead of trying to come up with a large amount all at once. Most of us resort to using a credit card because the latter didn't happen and then we're back to paying off debt. It's a vicious cycle.

One of the most common questions asked by my community is, "what are my three favorite cash envelopes?" My answer was easy: Christmas, vacations, and Target.

Cheap people exhibit stinginess, focusing solely on minimizing expenses without regard for value or enjoyment. They may go to extremes to avoid spending money, such as excessively haggling over small amounts or refusing to contribute their fair share in group settings.

GENEROSITY VERSUS SELFISHNESS

The frugal understands the importance of balancing saving with generosity and giving back to others. They may budget for charitable donations or thoughtful gifts, recognizing the positive impact of helping others and building meaningful relationships.

The cheap prioritize their savings above all else, often at the expense of others. They may exhibit selfish behavior, such as refusing to contribute to shared expenses or expecting others to cover their costs, undermining trust and goodwill in relationships.

LIFESTYLE VERSUS DEPRIVATION FRUGAL

Individuals adopt a sustainable lifestyle that allows them to live comfortably within their means while still enjoying life's pleasures. They may find creative ways to cut costs without sacrificing happiness or fulfillment, such as cooking meals at home or participating in free or low-cost activities.

Cheap individuals view saving money as a form of deprivation or sacrifice, leading to a constant focus on scarcity and limitations. They may avoid spending money altogether, even when it would enhance their quality of life or well-being, leading to feelings of deprivation and discontent.

BENEFITS OF A FRUGAL LIFESTYLE

Now that we can distinguish between the two, what are the benefits of being frugal, and why would someone choose this way of life?

Stability and freedom. When you spend where you value, you feel financial stability. You also experience freedom in knowing where your money goes and that you had control over it went. There's freedom in having a plan. Without a plan, there's stress, anxiety, and uncertainty. We have enough situations where we have those feelings in other areas. We do not need to feel them when it comes to our money.

Increased Savings and Investments. In this season of life, we must maximize the amount of money coming in to give us the best return. We are investing in our future, and there's no more time to play games. Saving is the new game in town, and there's no option *but* to win.

Reduced Environmental Impact. If you care about our world and want to leave it in better condition than how you found it, being frugal and green go hand in hand. "Use it up, wear it out, make it do, or do without," is a slogan that became popular during World War II. It is the anthem of the frugal people and benefits the earth.

Improved Quality of Life. Once we control spending our money in areas we value, while cutting back on things we don't value as much, we are free to pursue the things we love the most. Whether that means more traveling or community giving, frugality allows you to allocate those resources toward activities, hobbies, and foundations about which you're passionate.

Frugal living may also lead to a healthier life. Examples include cooking at home instead of fast food and participating in free or low-cost activities, including exercising. Playing games at home and in-home movies for entertainment rather than going out to the movies and paying for other entertainment activities. Of course, this means many movies already were released, but it also means a closer trip to the bathroom and far less expensive snacks!

Frugality can foster community engagement by promoting sharing, bartering, volunteering, and supporting local businesses. A greater sense of community leads to stronger social connections and a love for the people around you.

Greater Flexibility. As you practice frugality, you see debt decrease and finally disappear. Once the lenders don't have you handcuffed and chained to your debt, you get to choose where you want to work and whether you want to work. There's financial flexibility when you don't owe anyone anything. There's also financial flexibility to handle unexpected expenses or to pursue opportunities that sat on the back burner due to tight finances.

I love that financial freedom allows me to help my family whenever possible. Next year, I'm paying for my granddaughter to take dance lessons. My Gram did it for me, and now I can do it for Mae. Plus, baby number three will have arrived by then, so I know they could use a little break financially, and Mae will benefit from dance lessons.

Now that we've got the business of budgets out of the way and understand what being frugal is about, we can get to the super fun stuff—getting down to the nitty-gritty of frugality!

Always remember kindness comes first; we are all here to serve each other!

6
MONEY'S TRUE POWER

CONTENTMENT, FULFILLMENT, AND FREEDOM

"A big part of financial freedom is having your heart
and mind free from worry about the what-ifs of life."

Suze Orman

Mindset seems to be an overused trendy word this decade, and I feel like it scares people off. If you don't want to sound woo-woo or hokey, instead of mindset, you could call it *thoughts* or *beliefs*. I prefer to use mindset.

When you change your mind or shift your thoughts to places of gratitude, contentment, empowerment, resourcefulness, and/or internal fulfillment, you will be shocked (shocked, I say) to feel the shift that happens. Dread, fear, spending, and comparison all just disappear.

When we explore the topic of frugal living, not only as an entire lifestyle change, but as a means to an end, it can sound ominous. I'm talking about the end of your working life or career, not the other *final end*. A change of mindset is imperative.

I LOVE self-development. I am a nerd for any book or videocast (a podcast recorded and put on YouTube) that deals with being a better human, earning more money, or tapping into the world beyond my own little bubble.

So, when I come across a mindset concept that allows me to listen to my thoughts and gives me the tools to change those thoughts, behaviors, and paradigms that are engrained in my past from my environment, I am all in—and I mean *jumping* in with both feet!

Changing your thoughts about money can significantly impact your financial life and happiness. When you adopt a positive and growth-oriented money mindset, you start to feel more in control of your finances and make choices that align with your goals. Instead of seeing budgeting and saving as restrictive, you begin to view them as tools that open up opportunities for your future. This change in perspective reduces financial stress and anxiety, helping you focus on abundance rather than feeling stuck in scarcity. When you're confident in your ability to manage money, the constant worry about financial security starts to fade, giving you a genuine sense of peace.

One of the most extraordinary things about having a positive money mindset is that it helps you see opportunities where you once saw obstacles. This open-minded approach encourages you to be innovative and find new ways to increase your income and/or reduce expenses. Plus, you're more likely to seek learning opportunities and connect with people who can offer valuable financial insights, further broadening your horizons and options.

Improving your money mindset can also do wonders for your relationships. Open and honest conversations about finances are vital to maintaining healthy relationships with family and partners. By fostering a mindset that values transparency, you can work together towards shared financial goals, strengthening your bond and mutual understanding. This collaborative spirit extends to other parts of life, where you can align your spending with your values, leading to greater satisfaction and happiness.

Had I understood this years ago when I was newly married, instead of believing that I would be weak to admit that I was a terrible money manager, I may have stopped the bullet train before it hit the wall.

Being resilient is another great perk of having a solid money mindset. When financial challenges pop up, a growth-oriented mindset helps you adapt and find solutions, keeping you focused on long-term goals instead of getting bogged down by short-term setbacks. This resiliency is essential in today's ever-changing financial world, allowing you to navigate changes confidently.

Ultimately, having a positive money mindset is about cultivating abundance and opening yourself up to a world of possibilities. It helps you break free from negative beliefs about money you might have picked up along the way and create a healthier financial future. By shifting your focus from scarcity to abundance, you empower yourself to build a financial legacy for your family and community, ensuring security and opportunities for future generations.

Changing your money mindset also sparks personal growth. It encourages continuous learning and adaptation, fostering an environment where you can focus on self-improvement. By prioritizing experiences and relationships over material possessions, you align your spending with what truly matters, leading to greater fulfillment and happiness.

Changing your money mindset is a powerful step toward achieving financial freedom and personal fulfillment.

Adopting a positive, growth-oriented perspective empowers you to achieve your goals, reduce stress, and live a life aligned with your values and aspirations. This shift enhances your financial well-being and enriches every part of your life, enabling you to live a more fulfilled and abundant life. By embracing a positive money mindset, you unlock the potential to transform your financial future and create a lasting impact on yourself and those around you.

SHIFT FROM INSTANT GRATIFICATION TO LONG-TERM SATISFACTION

In consumer culture, many women prioritize instant gratification through material possessions and experiences. We all know what the Facebook Feeds and Instagram Reels of that person who just returned from a lavish tropical vacation look like.

Women in midlife are transitioning toward a more frugal lifestyle, shifting their focus from their immediate desires to their long-term satisfaction. Setting and achieving big goals feels much better than those new boots! We can acknowledge that impulse purchases lead to financial strain, heartache, and overpowering guilt in the long run.

Reframing your mindset (or changing your thoughts) toward long-term goals like financial stability, debt freedom, or a semi-early retirement can help you resist the temptations of overspending.

PIVOT FROM COMPARISON TO CONTENTMENT

Midlife often raises awareness of societal expectations and comparisons. These expectations and comparisons drive the spending habits bus we hop on to maintain appearances. We are aging, maybe gaining some weight (thank you, menopause), and getting a little grey hair here and there.

Society tells us that midlife women are not what they used to be, and we need to fight like heck not to show our age. We compare ourselves to those who are around our age and look fantastic. I'm talking to you, Jennifer Aniston, and J. Lo.

These comparisons leak into our finances. Not only are we spending more money to dye our hair and invest in the latest face serums, but we are looking at others wondering how they can afford that Mercedes or that vacation when you might be struggling to take care of everyone and pay off that water heater that pooped the bed three months ago.

The good news is we can recognize the value of simplicity and a more minimalist approach. We have the wisdom to understand that fulfillment isn't derived from material possessions or outdoing others.

True satisfaction lies in meaningful relationships, personal growth, experiences that align with our values, and being in a place financially where we can feel the release of the money burden dissolve off our shoulders, freeing us up to enjoy our best years.

You find contentment in living within your means rather than indulging in trending joys.

TRANSFER FROM FEAR TO EMPOWERMENT

Transitioning to a frugal lifestyle may seem daunting (gosh, my friend Jill, a fellow blogger and brilliant copywriter, really dislikes the word "daunting" and so each time I use it, I giggle and think of her). It may seem terrifying, particularly for women facing debt or financial insecurities. However, if you allow it, these thought shifts can empower you, shifting from fear and anxiety about money to a sense of superhero status and control.

Frugality is recognized not as deprivation yet as an *intentional* choice aligning with your priorities and values. Alignment means that when you choose to be frugal, you show your values through where you spend your money. If you value expensive-looking purses, luxury cars, and big houses, that's where all your money will go, whether you have money or not. If you value family trips to the beach, backyard summer gatherings, and holiday parties, that's where you'll spend. if you value a paid-off house, a car with no payments, and a nice retirement nest egg, well, guess what?!

Taking control of your finances, setting achievable goals, and adopting sensible spending habits instill confidence in shaping your financial future.

SWIVEL FROM CONSUMERISM TO RESOURCEFULNESS

Moving away from consumerism into a life of resourcefulness is a natural progression when you have goals. As we age, we come to terms with what we find necessary. Keeping up with The Jones next door is no longer a way to express our individuality. Not caring what others think about you is a rite of passage.

As a society, we are moving away from equating success and happiness with material possessions. Instead of solely relying on buying new items for the sake of status, we appreciate our ability to be creative and use items we already have.

This shift in mindset and behavior encourages exploration of DIY projects, repurposing belongings, and finding cost-effective solutions. It doesn't mean hopping on your phone and ordering from Amazon same-day delivery.

REDIRECT FROM EXTERNAL VALIDATION TO INTERNAL FULFILLMENT

Most individuals seek validation through material possessions or social status. A frugal lifestyle transition entails shifting from seeking external validation to finding fulfillment internally.

We don't care as much about what people think of us. We are coming into an age where we know who we are, what we like, and what (and who) is important to us. We realize happiness comes from aligning our spending habits with our values and priorities.

Instead of conforming to societal expectations, we focus more on personal growth, self-care, and take time to pursue our passions. This shift redefines our definition of success. We decide to focus on ourselves and our loved ones. This creates room for beautiful experiences rather than purchasing possessions.

ENVISION YOUR RETIREMENT LIFESTYLE

Defining your desired retirement lifestyle means deciding where you will live, how often you will travel, what your hobbies will be, how far away you want to be from family, and, of course, the critical yet expensive need for healthcare.

Spend some time considering the high cost of health care and what that would look like for you, specifically if retirement comes before you qualify for Medicare at 65. Also, don't forget to factor in inflation and changes to your income sources.

SET YOUR GOALS

Now is the time to break out a Google Doc or a notebook because it is more effective when your goals are written down and you see them in black and white. I suggest you keep a goal-specific notebook, since something truly happens in the brain when you put pen to paper, making the hand/brain connection.

Establishing clear and achievable financial goals means that it's time to define the target retirement age you're aiming for and your desired income. How much will you need to live on? Just basic living expenses, such as home maintenance, utilities, food, transportation, and potential healthcare costs, just to name a few. Next, add any discretionary spending—all the fun stuff like travel, hobbies, gifts, and anything else you'd like to do or start doing during your golden years.

Consider Specific, Measurable, Achievable, Relevant, and Time-bound (SMART) goals. A SMART goal is a clear and structured way to set easily understood and achievable objectives.

1. **Specific:** This means your goal should be clear and specific. Instead of saying, "I want to save money," you would say, "I want to save $500 for a vacation to Walt Disney World." The more detailed your goal, the better you'll know what you're aiming for.

2. **Measurable:** You need a way to track your progress. If you aim to save $500, you can measure how much you save each week or month, and it helps you stay on track and see how far you've come.

3. **Achievable:** Your goal should be realistic and attainable. Setting a goal to save $1,000 monthly when you only have $100 left after expenses isn't achievable. Make sure your goal is something you can reasonably accomplish with the resources and time you have.

4. **Relevant:** Your goal should matter to you and align with other plans in your life. If you prioritize reducing stress and enjoying a break, saving for a vacation is relevant. You're less likely to stay motivated if your goal doesn't fit your bigger picture.

5. **Time-bound:** Finally, setting a deadline for your goal creates a sense of urgency and helps you stay focused. For example, saying, "I want to save $500 in the next six months" gives a clear timeframe within which to work.

So, when you set SMART goals, you're giving yourself a clear, trackable, and realistic roadmap, making it much more likely that you'll achieve your goal.

At the end of the day, money is just a tool—it's how you use it that matters. When you focus on finding contentment, seeking fulfillment, and embracing freedom, you'll discover that true wealth isn't just about numbers, but the joy and peace it brings. Remember, it's not about having it all; it's about living fully with what you have.

7

FRUGAL FOOD CHOICES

HEALTHY MEALS, BUDGET-FRIENDLY STRATEGIES

"Good food should be a right and not a privilege.
It should be affordable and available to everyone."

Alice Waters

Food is the next most expensive basic need after housing and maybe medical. We need to hone our grocery and food budget skills to reach our goals, get out of debt, save for retirement, and enjoy our lives. Food prices continue to increase, and they will never return to pre-covid prices.

According to the United States Department of Agriculture (USDA), in June 2019, the average cost of groceries to feed a family of four (two adults and two children between the ages of six and eight) on a moderate grocery budget was $1,065.20 per month.

In June 2024, the same family on a moderate food budget paid $1,273.52.

If you've ever had growing children in your home, then you are aware that as children grow, so does your grocery budget. Athletes in the home can impact the budget even more.

The following are a few ideas to help manage your food budget better.

PLAN MEALS

Meal planning and preparation are essential for lowering the food budget. Benjamin Franklin once said, "If you fail to plan, you are planning to fail." Essential—I say ESSENTIAL!

Plan weekly meals on a computer program, a chalkboard in your kitchen, or the back of a junk mail envelope on your refrigerator. It doesn't matter where—just not only in your head. There's way too much going on there to keep it all straight.

Pick one day specifically for meal planning. Review your inventory to see what you already have, and plan meals around those existing items first. These two tips will minimize food waste, use up what you already have, and save you money.

I always look to see what I have and plan from there first. For example, as I opened the freezer, I noticed a package of chicken wings that came in one of those meat delivery boxes I tried two months ago—we need to eat those soon. I also saw thin-cut pork chops, ground beef, and the leftover sauce that my youngest got with the pizza pinwheels that he didn't finish.

So, our dinner meal plan for the week includes chicken wings twice, a pot of chili enough for two meals, and ranch pork chops (pork chops dipped in ranch dressing first, then breadcrumbs, and cooked in our cast iron pan).

We already have beans for the chili, spices, sauce, and ranch dressing.

CREATE A LIST

Next, list any ingredients needed to fill in the holes.

I will need more meat for another meal, so I make a note to check the *loss leaders* when at the store for a good sale. This strategy is a great way to keep the budget low. How about a pasta dish? Pasta dishes are always a frugal way to go. A fun frugal formula for pasta dishes might look like this:

1. *Pick a pasta*. It might be angel hair, farfalle, or elbow.
2. *Add a protein*. If you have chicken left over, throw that in. Grab a can of beans. Garbanzo or cannellini (white kidney beans) are two of my favorites for pasta. Ground beef or sausage will also work.
3. *Choose a sauce*. Red tomato sauce, white alfredo sauce, or a lemon butter sauce all taste delish.
4. *Sneak in some veggies*. We love chicken, broccoli, and sun-dried tomatoes in a lemon butter sauce over angel hair for a quick and frugal meal.

I also will need breadcrumbs or a generic/store-brand Shake-n-Bake, sauce for the wings, frozen veggies, and other side dishes.

If you are like me and tend to use the same things every week, for example: eggs, bacon, spinach, and yogurt, then add those items to the list.

Check for sales online and/or the newspaper—if you still receive it at home—before you get to the store. Look for loss leaders and other sales on the things you already need. If you're not partial to brands, you can decide on the bacon based on the sale instead of the brand, allowing you to save a little.

There are many ways to create a list. One idea is to print out a weekly pre-typed list, keep it attached to the refrigerator, then circle what you need to replace.

You can find a free copy of the grocery list I love at <u>frozenpennies. com/fun.</u>

My daughter-in-law, Krystan, asks *Alexa* to add it to the grocery list, so she can follow it on her phone app when she gets to the store. What works for me is to keep a master list on my phone using my Notes app, so when I need something, I add it there. Searching the App Store on your phone will find several choices to fit your needs.

Remember to check your store app for coupons as well ahead of time, not as you're standing at the register ready to check out!

EMBRACE BATCH COOKING AND MEAL PREP

If you cook in bulk and portion out meals, you will always have ready-made meals, eliminating or at least reducing the need for last-minute take out or delivery. If you still have a houseful of people, portioning meals might not work as well but cooking more at one time to use in multiple dishes, such as: casseroles, sandwiches, salads, and soup, absolutely will help you save time and money. Batch cooking sides in advance, such as rice and pasta will save time for those soups, casseroles, as well as other dishes throughout the week.

An example of this from the above meal plan would be the chili. It's a big pot that anybody can eat for two separate dinners or frozen in single portions for later. Usually, when I make chili, we eat it in a bowl one night, have it as nachos another night, and still have enough left to freeze for two lunches or another round of nachos.

We are utilizing leftovers creatively by incorporating them into subsequent meals, without eating the exact same meal. By changing one or two items, we keep it more interesting. Don't forget your BFF, the freezer. Having leftover veggies after dinner each night and throwing them in a container in the freezer will give you a delicious addition to a soup. An excellent reminder is to record the item with a date on the freezer bag or container. If you're like me, you could forget what it is and definitely how old it is.

My mom did this, but with everything leftover. If there was a little pasta left, it went into the freezer bowl. Half a pork chop? Freezer bowl. Rice, pasta, barley? Yup. Freezer bowl. When the freezer bowl was full, she would add stock and make soup out of all the leftovers. It was some of the best soup I ever ate. She called it freezer soup and it was different every time.

If just one or two of you still live at home, meal prep containers will save your sanity and wallet. One day a week, preparing three to four different larger meals to pack up for lunch and dinner will allow you to cut back on take-out *and* be healthier.

CHOOSE COST-EFFECTIVE INGREDIENTS

Choose budget-friendly ingredients such as grains, legumes, and seasonal produce to keep your budget in check. Rice and beans are a super inexpensive option. If you add some corn and salsa, you can call it a burrito bowl.

Explore other protein sources, such as: beans, tofu, tempeh, or eggs to reduce meat costs. Seek out meat markdowns and make friends with the butcher behind the meat counter so they can fill you in on the days and times the meat gets marked down.

Purchase generic or store-brand products instead of national brands. I can tell you that Aldi's brand organic ketchup is good, maybe even better, than Heinz! If you don't have Aldi in your area, try other low-cost stores, if you haven't already.

In the first chapter, I talked about my Mama's garden. For a few dollars in seeds or starter plants, you can have a glorious bounty every late summer or early fall, depending on your part of the country. Initially, there will be a start-up cost, but the payoff will be grand, delicious, and healthy!

Learning how to preserve that harvest is a necessity. You will see the savings if you, like Mama, can pickles, veggies, jams, and fruits—she even cans her own apple cider vinegar and homemade vanilla extract.

We have a container garden this year with a few cucumber plants, tomatoes, and lettuce. It's not enough to feed the family all year, yet just enough for fresh tomato sandwiches and several salads. At least it's a start. I hope to grow it just a bit each year—*pun intended!* Even small containers placed on a windowsill for spinach leaves or herbs can help reduce grocery costs!

BE FLEXIBLE AND RESOURCEFUL

My local library has a program called *Farm to Library*. The library has a small refrigerator, and shelves, which are filled once a week with local goodies. It's free for anyone who wants or needs it. I have checked it out and have seen items, such as: eggs, honey, bread, vegetables, and fruit. There could be a similar program in your area to help reduce food waste.

Adapt recipes to use what you already have in your home. If the recipe calls for rice but you have quinoa, use that instead. Would ground beef work if it calls for chicken and you're fresh out? Most of the time, recipes can be adapted to make use of what is readily available in your house without purchasing more.

Incorporate pantry staples and leftovers into your meals first to avoid throwing good food away. Experiment with versatile ingredients and simple cooking techniques to create delicious, budget-friendly meals. The internet is jam-packed with ideas. Involve your family, especially young kids, and turn it into a cooking adventure. If kids have a part in meal prep, they are more likely to eat the meal and/or try new things.

PRIORITIZE NUTRIENT-RICH FOODS

I understand that those on special diets may have more of a challenge than those who don't, but if you can still eat whole foods and ingredients instead of processed, prepackaged foods, you just might get more bang for your buck.

Focus on meals higher in protein and nutrient-rich ingredients, opt for simple and versatile recipes, such as whole grains, lean protein, paired with colorful fruits and vegetables. Remember to add in healthy fats. They will make you feel satiated for longer and are good for brain health. Consider nuts, seeds, and healthy oils to enhance flavor and satiety. Don't forget most everyone's favorite—it's mine for sure—the avocado.

Experiment with herbs, spices, and other seasonings to add flavor to dishes without relying on expensive ingredients, unhealthy additives, and luxury spices—whatever those are! This is where your home-grown herbs come in handy.

OPT FOR SIMPLE AND VERSATILE RECIPES

I'm not a fun cook. I don't care about cooking, but because I'm frugal, I cannot do anything else. Uber Eats is WAY too expensive and doesn't deliver to my tiny town. So, I choose to cook. However, my meals are simple: meat, potatoes, veggies, casseroles, soups, sheet pan dishes, and skillet meals, are just about the extent of my repertoire.

When I look for a new recipe, it has to be easy and fast with minimal ingredients. Otherwise, I'll be having pizza delivered (which is the only thing we can get delivered in my tiny town). Plan meals to avoid delivery and have the ingredients on hand for a quick dinner. Tacos, spaghetti with meatballs, frozen soup, and grilled cheese sandwiches are inexpensive, and even better, they are fast.

Experiment with one-pot meals, stir-fry, salads with homemade dressings, and soups that anyone can easily customize for individual tastes and personal preferences. You can create a similar thing with stir fry that my Mama did to create her Freezer Soup. Just add leftover meat and veggies to a pan with some soy sauce, spices, herbs if you like, then serve with rice or pasta.

Look for those recipes that require minimal ingredients and preparation time to streamline the cooking process.

SHOP SEASONAL

Shopping according to what is in abundance during each season not only means shopping for fruits and vegetables that are in season, yet also means stocking up around the holidays. Condiments almost always go on sale for the July Fourth holiday, so buy enough to get you through the year. Around Thanksgiving, turkeys are a great price. If you have freezer space, get two or three.

Roadside stands and farmers markets can be great places to get low-cost produce and definitely very fresh. Our farmers' markets are not cheap, so instead I stop at local roadside stands for fruit and veggies. A friend likes to visit her farmers' market at the end of the day. She says the farmers are much more willing to give her a deal on produce (even in bulk), so they don't have to load it back up on the truck and take it home.

You could also post an announcement on your Facebook page letting friends know that you are willing to take their excess garden surplus.

Making frugal food choices doesn't mean you must sacrifice flavor or nutrition. With a little planning and creativity, you can enjoy delicious meals while keeping your budget in check. It's more about finding what works for you and making the most of every dollar spent. Keep experimenting, stay mindful, and have fun exploring all the tasty, frugal healthy options.

For free meal planning resources please visit my website at frozenpennies.com/fun.

8

FIT AND FABULOUS

STRENGTH FOR THE SECOND ACT

"Age is just a number, but keeping your body active
keeps your mind sharp. It's important
to stay physically engaged in life."

Betty White

I've discovered a new passion in my 50s. It's called taking care of myself—no time like the present to finally have a minute or two to put my health first. My family will definitely thank me later.

Tragically, my dad passed away in 2018 from complications of a heart attack. Four months before that, my mom had a heart attack. She's doing great, but heart issues run in my family. Even though this familial threat has been weighing heavy on my heart, *pun intended*, I have done very little to commit to a program that will benefit my own heart health.

I like to say that I've tried all diets and exercise programs, and while I probably have tried many—I just never stuck to anything long enough to make positive changes. I finally decided to do just that. I have consulted with a nutritionist, have eliminated sugar, get good sleep, drink lots of water, and walk regularly. It's the cheapest form of good exercise out there. I also have begun to add in weight training since it helps increase bone strength and muscle mass that we lose as we age. Hopefully, this will increase our chances of being strong and agile enough to get up off the floor on our own in our older years.

MULTIFUNCTIONAL EQUIPMENT

If you require more than that to get healthy, let's explore some affordable home workout equipment. Look for equipment that can target multiple muscle groups and offer a variety of exercises. Consider purchasing inexpensive items like resistance bands, dumbbells, and kettlebells, which are all small, compact, and easy to store. They also provide a range of resistance levels for different fitness requirements.

Know that resistance bands are affordable even when purchased new. You often can find weights inexpensively at thrift shops, online marketplaces like Facebook, Craigslist, buy-nothing groups, and garage sales. Ask around. Someone might already have exercise gadgets that they are no longer using and would love to unload it.

BUDGET FRIENDLY GYMS, FITNESS APPS, AND ONLINE RESOURCES

If you need to get out of the house and be social, many chain gyms are affordable. Places like the YMCA and Planet Fitness are less expensive and offer flexible hours. Research discounts they might offer, such as: veterans, student, teacher discounts, and senior discounts. Check into your insurance to see if they offer a stipend for members as well.

My friend, Michelle, was a single mom who loved working out, so she secured a second job teaching fitness classes every Saturday morning. So, not only did she earn an extra small paycheck, but her job included a free membership to the YMCA. This was a win-win all around.

Consider your local school. Our high school is open five evenings a week to allow for walking indoors during the cold season. It is free of charge and incorporates a warm, dry place to get moving, complete with stairs. In the steamy hot south, many folks make use of indoor malls to walk. Walking with someone also is more motivating than alone. The talking makes the time pass very quickly. A walking date is free, and healthy for mind, body, and soul.

One of my favorite places to find great exercise videos is YouTube. I discovered walk-inside videos and use them at times that I can't walk outside due to inclement weather. I first discovered these free online programs when I had a wicked pulled muscle in my calf, and tackling the hills in my neighborhood just about brought me to tears. I could turn down the volume and pop in Foo Fighters while I walked in place for 30 minutes.

Searching Pinterest also can yield some great ideas regarding at-home workouts. Many of the creators that have free plans also have low-cost paid plans with more details or more robust programs. Instagram and TikTok are also valuable platforms on which to discover new ideas.

You can find everything from yoga to walking to High Intensity Interval Training (HIIT) online. Many of these programs offer body wight exercises or routines that require minimal equipment, making them not only accessible yet affordable, as well.

DIY HOME GYM

Create a DIY home gym if you have the space using inexpensive or repurposed items around your house.

- Refill milk jugs with sand for a weight that works for you and slowly add to it as you make progress.
- Use a sturdy chair for seated exercises, incline pushups, or triceps dips.
- Fill reusable bags with books or canned goods to use as weights.
- Use a jump rope for cardio.
- Shop second-hand sales for other equipment that you might need at a fraction of the cost of brand new.

Whatever you choose, just remember that incorporating healthy physical activity can help keep costs down by minimizing health issues that require a doctor visit.

Being fit and fabulous isn't about perfection; it's about feeling strong and confident in this next chapter of life. Embrace the journey, listen to your body, and celebrate the little wins along the way. You're building strength not just for today, but for a lifetime of enjoying all the moments that matter most.

9

MINDFUL AND MONEYWISE

SELF-CARE ON A BUDGET

"Almost everything will work again if you unplug it for
a few minutes, including you."

Anne Lamott

The term self-care may come across as trendy, but when you
have lived your life caring for others all the time, it's a good
reminder that we also need to care for ourselves. I now often find
that a dull, boring day with nothing pressing on my schedule can
be one of my best days. I LOVE to be bored! It doesn't happen
that often though.

This is especially true for women. We tend to be the primary
caregivers for everyone, including partners, children,
grandchildren, and aging parents. Women often juggle home
upkeep, careers, cooking, kids, and most of the family planning.
I recognize that while men *can* and *do* take on these roles,

traditionally it has fallen on more women than men. One big difference is that women in midlife must deal with the effects of menopause which can be quite unpleasant and can make life in general more complicated.

There are many ways that women in midlife may practice self-care. When googled, the typical responses are to take a hot bath, get a massage, and have a mani/pedi, but there seems to be so much more to self-care for me. You may already be doing things you might not even realize are genuine, authentic self-care, like reading this book. *Thank you by the way!*

Let's go into a few great ideas of self-care that you may have yet to think about.

GOOD SLEEP HYGIENE

Good sleep is one form of self-care I've been working on for quite some time. As I mentioned earlier, I went through menopause early at 35, and since then, my sleep has been a dumpster fire. Last year, I splurged on good quality blackout blinds for my bedroom windows. It was my Christmas gift to myself. They are super bougie with remote controls. I covered all devices in my bedroom that emitted light. I'm not sure why it's necessary for everything that plugs in to have a little light. It makes me super crazy.

The following are a few great tips I've discovered on my sleep journey:

- Establish a consistent schedule and stick to it. For me, it means to be in bed by 9:30 p.m. every night, with 30 minutes of reading, and lights out at 10 p.m. sharp. My alarm is set for 6:20 a.m.

- Create a relaxing bedtime routine. Avoid screens for at least an hour before bed. Consider gentle stretches, a warm shower or bath, and journaling.

- Minimize screen time (and yes, I'm repeating this again because it's *that* important), dim all the lights in your home, reduce noise, and create a cool, dark place for you to lay your head and eventually drift off to sleep with sweet dreams.

Also, for my female audience, speak to your doctor about perimenopause. Your hormones can start going a little wonky in your 30s. If you are having trouble sleeping and have done everything the expert says to do, it might be worth the trip to go deeper.

Since I went through menopause early, took hormone replacement therapy, and then stopped once my symptoms disappeared (when I thought I didn't need it any longer), I feel like this may be the root of the sleep issues I've had for more than a decade. Boy, I wish I knew what I know now; I never would have stopped.

Chat with your doctor, and don't put a Band-Aid on it. Find the source of the problem and then establish a plan.

PRACTICE MINDFULNESS AND MEDITATION

I don't know about you, but I always heard the word mindfulness and had zero idea what it meant. So, I took some time to research and found that it means being focused and tuned into what you're doing. If you are eating breakfast, don't be thinking about what you're going to have for dinner, how your son needs to get that college essay written by Friday, and that you need to remind your husband (again) that the oil really needs to be changed on the car 1,500 miles ago. Concentrate on breakfast—the combination of the sweet and the tart flavor of the yogurt, the burst and juiciness of the blueberries as you bite into them, and the firm crunch of the granola and nuts.

As you wash dishes and pots, smell the dish soap, notice the shininess of the saucepan, see the bubbles in the sink, and feel the water's warmth. I know that in a crazy, fast-paced world where distraction is prominent, there's a constant bombardment of information, social media apps—enough to scroll your life away—and never-ending to-do lists, it's easy to feel overwhelmed and disconnected.

Mindfulness offers an opportunity for us to pause and reconnect, helping us focus on the present instead of getting caught up in the chaos around us. Mindfulness can reduce stress, improve mental clarity, and enhance overall well-being. It encourages us to take a step back, breathe, and appreciate the little things in life, helping us find balance and peace amid the hustle and bustle. There never seems to be a break in our lives these days, since everything is so immediate.

Mindfulness helps us become more aware of our thoughts and feelings without judgment, which can lead to better emotional regulation and reduced anxiety. It allows us to break free from negative thought patterns and fosters a greater sense of self-compassion and empathy. By being mindful, we can approach challenges with a calmer and more focused mindset, making navigating life's ups and downs easier.

Today's society has made practicing mindfulness even more crucial. With technology constantly demanding our attention, it's easy to become distracted and lose touch with what truly matters. Mindfulness encourages us to unplug and be present, allowing us to engage in our relationships and experiences fully. It reminds us to slow down, savor the moment, and prioritize our mental and emotional health. In a world where outside gurus often praise multitasking, mindfulness teaches us the value of doing one thing at a time and being fully present, leading to more meaningful and fulfilling interactions.

Learn to meditate and set aside time for it every day. Most people who say they cannot meditate are the ones who need it the most.

I recently watched Lewis Howes on YouTube interview Jenna Zoe, a world-leading expert in Human Design. For those like me who had no idea what Human Design is, it's a little like astrology, but with a holistic approach. I was intrigued by the interview; so, I did some more research into the Human Design concept. Reading more about it, I learned that depending on when you were born, you have characteristics and traits that are different from everyone else. Through this research, I learned that light stops thoughts from spinning. So, when I feel stressed, anxious, or overwhelmed, I seek out sunlight. When working inside, I use a softer light source. As I was reading that, I thought, "DANG! This is so true!" I have two light sconces in my office, and one of the light bulbs remains unscrewed because both provide too much light for me.

When I need to get out of my head, I sit in the yard or take the afternoon to float in the pool. Winter is a little more challenging, but even bundling up and stepping outside to feel the sun on my face helps a bit.

For the last few years, I made it a priority to save money all year long to get away to Florida in February, the middle of cold winter days for us. It has been a game changer for my mental health. I know not everyone can do this, so stepping outside even on the coldest, greyest days is better than nothing.

GROUNDING

There is something that I've learned recently called grounding and it's more than just a trend.

Grounding, or earthing, is all about connecting with the earth's natural energy to boost physical and emotional well-being. Think of it as a way to recharge your body by making direct contact with the earth, which has a subtle electrical charge. You can do this by walking barefoot on grass, soil, sand, or using grounding mats indoors that mimic the earth's natural electric current and allow you to bring the experience into your home when walking barefoot outside is not an option.

HOW GROUNDING WORKS

The earth is a natural source of electrons, believed to have antioxidant effects that can neutralize free radicals in the body. When you contact the ground, these electrons are thought to transfer to your body, helping to balance your internal electrical state. This connection reduces inflammation, improves sleep, and enhances overall well-being.

Benefits of Grounding:

- *Reduced inflammation.* Grounding might help decrease inflammation by neutralizing free radicals linked to chronic diseases and aging.

- *Improved sleep.* Many people report better sleep and more restful nights after grounding, thanks to its calming effects on the nervous system.

- *Enhanced mood.* Grounding can promote calmness and relaxation, reducing stress and anxiety.

- *Increased energy.* By balancing your body's electrical state, grounding can lead to more vitality and energy.

- *Pain reduction.* Some studies suggest that grounding can help alleviate pain and discomfort, especially for those with chronic pain conditions.

If you're looking for a simple and natural way to feel more grounded, balanced, and energized, why not try grounding?

ENGAGE IN PHYSICAL ACTIVITY

Find time in your schedule to incorporate regular physical exercise. Being more physical has numerous health benefits, including boosting mood and reducing anxiety. Take advantage of free or low-cost fitness options like walking, jogging, or cycling outside. Many cities and towns offer classes in the park, like yoga or low-intensity aerobics. Walking is the least expensive exercise. Go for a walk. Break it up throughout the day in 10-minute blocks or do one long walk in the evening with a friend.

Even the smallest things, like parking further away, climbing the stairs as much as you can, or doing one to two more laps around the grocery store, will add up. I addressed finding inexpensive ways to incorporate physical activity in an earlier chapter. There are really no excuses why NOT to have a more physical lifestyle.

NOURISH YOUR BODY WITH NUTRIENT-RICH FOODS

Prioritize nourishing your body with only the foods that serve you well. Whole, nutrient-dense foods that support overall health and well-being. Michael Pollan, author of *In Defense of Food* and *The Omnivore's Dilemma* shares, "Eat real foods, mostly plants." If you're cutting out processed foods and snacks, you will find that your grocery budget doesn't change as much as you might think.

If you're trying to get out of debt, this might be disappointing, but you will save money down the line since you will save on health care costs.

Plan and prepare budget-friendly meals at home using affordable ingredients like whole grains, beans, lean meats, and vegetables. Add fruit as a sweet ending to a meal. Experiment with new recipes and cooking techniques to make healthy eating enjoyable and sustainable. The internet is FULL of great and exciting recipes.

Be aware of your own body. The internet and social media are full of experts telling you which diet will make you live the longest. Consider what foods work and what foods do not work for you, since all of us have different tolerances.

I am NOT good with sugar or anything that turns into sugar, like bread or wine (yes, I see the biblical reference here). I have to be super careful with my cheese and dairy consumption, and I need to eat at least 30 grams of protein three times a day to feel optimal. It took me a hot minute to figure this out. I encourage you to do the same if you haven't already.

FOSTER CONNECTION AND SOCIAL SUPPORT

Cultivate meaningful connections with friends, family, or community members to foster a sense of belonging and support. Prioritize quality time with loved ones through activities like shared meals, walks, or creative outlets. Seek free or low-cost social activities and events in your community to expand your social network and enhance your spirit.

These suggestions might be more appealing to my extrovert reader. However, if you consider yourself as an introvert yet still want to foster a connection with your community and meet new people, you might consider stepping outside of your comfort zone, but on your terms.

With most of us being so busy with our own lives, you might need to reach out to friends and family and set up a potluck, coffee date, or walking club.

EMBRACE NATURE AND OUTDOOR TIME

I've been doing a lot of research lately on sleep and the effects of cortisol on increased anxiety (which can lead to sleep issues). One recurring suggestion is to get outside in the sun. In fact, going outside and feeling the sun on your face, as soon as you are awake can help sync your circadian rhythm.

Spending time outside in nature helps recharge and boost your mental, emotional, and physical well-being. Take advantage of free hiking, picnicking, or exploring local parks and nature trails. Connect with the natural world by skipping earbuds and for me, skipping Foo Fighters, to practice mindfulness outdoors. Observe wildlife, the world around you, or simply enjoy the beauty of your surroundings wherever you are. You can do this in the city by walking or on a nature trail in the desert. All that matters is that you are outside.

As we age, the need for friend interaction is super important. The introduction to social media in our culture has encouraged our society to communicate without physical interaction causing an increase in loneliness. There are many books and resources available regarding ways to become a better partner, parent, or child, but resources for being a better friend are not as plentiful, in my opinion.

Be a better friend to those in your life; if you don't have friends, find some.

If you are looking for new friends, consider volunteering for a cause close to your heart or joining a walking or book club. Use social media to your advantage to find groups that meet in person and welcome new members.

You can't be grateful and sad at the same time. *Or can you?* I like to think you can't, yet scientifically it is possible as emotions are super complex. For many, practicing gratitude does help.

Foster a positive mindset by practicing gratitude and focusing on the blessings in your life, no matter how small. Many people in this world do not even have the most basic life necessities, like clean water and safe shelter. There's always something for which to be grateful.

Start a gratitude journal to regularly reflect on and record things in your life for which you are thankful. Journaling is an excellent way to end your day as you relax before falling asleep. Writing positive thoughts creates a connection that differs from just saying it out loud. It hits differently.

Engage in positive affirmations and self-talk to counter the negative voice in your head. Create a more optimistic outlook on life. Even the most negative people can become more optimistic with time and practice, if they genuinely want to.

If you are on the journey to become debt-free, taking time for self-care may not be high on your priority list. However, it is important to remember that self-care and financial wellness can go hand in hand. For resources to help you balance both, please visit my website at frozenpennies.com/fun.

10
FRUGAL FASHIONISTA
LOOK FABULOUS WITHOUT THE SPLURGE

"Fashion you can buy, but style you possess. The key
to style is learning who you are, which takes years.
There's no how-to road map to style. It's about
self-expression and, above all, attitude."

Iris Apfel

While most of us are content to just look nice when heading out, some of us prefer trendy items and to feel stylish. I'm here to tell you that you can be trendy and stylish while remaining within your budget. If you're not one to shop for trendy fashion and love being frugal with your clothes to meet your goals, there are many ways to find what *fits* your comfort zone—pun intended.

ASSESS YOUR CURRENT WARDROBE

Take inventory of your wardrobe and identify essential and favorite pieces to determine what you genuinely love and wear regularly. You know that you have those go-to pieces that you wear often. In fact, statistically, we wear 20 percent of our clothes 80 percent of the time. One way to accomplish this seemingly overwhelming task is to completely empty your closet. Begin by putting back *first* the items you wear the most, then what you wear sometimes, and finally what you haven't worn in years, but are not ready to ditch. Don't put back clothes that you know you will *never* wear again.

Consider selling or donating unused items that no longer fit, are out of style (if that's something you care about), or no longer align with your personal needs. There are many different online avenues these days for selling clothing items, in addition to second-hand stores who will accept your items on consignment. However, if you itemize expenses for tax purposes, donating helps others while slightly decreasing your tax burden.

Many have mentioned that women's weight tends to fluctuate, and they think it's important to keep an array of clothing sizes, "just in case." I disagree. I'm more likely to maintain weight if the consequences of gaining weight mean I must buy more clothes. In fact, as I write this book, I am about halfway through my weight-loss journey. I'm getting rid of anything too big, and don't plan on ever wearing that size again.

If it does not fit or you don't feel great about yourself when wearing the item, take it out of your closet. We don't need that kind of negativity in our lives. Only keep what makes you feel great.

ADOPT A CAPSULE WARDROBE

Embrace the concept of a capsule wardrobe, which involves curating a small collection of essential clothing that works together and is worn interchangeably throughout the season. Choose a color pallet that compliments your style and ensures you can wear all pieces interchangeably. I love a good capsule wardrobe. I chose navy as my base color. So, most of my pieces can go with navy.

The following is an example of what a capsule wardrobe might contain:

- Jeans
- Tan or navy dress pants
- Tan or navy skirt
- White T-shirt
- Floral blouse
- Flannel shirt
- Two cardigans
- Dressy shoes
- Casual shoes

Wear the jeans with any of the tops. If it's chilly, add a cardigan. Wear any of the tops with the tan dress pants and dress it up or down with your choice of top plus accessories. Even just changing up your accessories with the same clothing items can change your style enough to break up the monotony.

PRIORITIZE QUALITY OVER QUANTITY

Build your minimalist wardrobe with versatile, timeless basics that you can mix and match to create various outfit combinations.

Invest in higher-quality staples such as well-fitting jeans, a classic white button shirt, neutral-colored tops, along with versatile dresses and suits.

Focus on well-made and durable pieces, rather than purchasing cheap, fast-fashion items that may quickly wear out or go out of style. Try to select natural, sustainable fabrics that wear well, are super comfortable, and easy to care for.

PRACTICE MINDFUL SPENDING HABITS

Before making a new clothing purchase, ask yourself whether the item aligns with your style, fits well, and fills a gap in your wardrobe. Avoid impulse shopping and instead opt for *intentional* purchases that add value to your wardrobe and contribute to a cohesive minimalist aesthetic.

Consider thrifting to fill those gaps or to construct that minimalist or capsule wardrobe. You can find some fantastic brands others no longer want or use.

- Research thrift stores in your area to find the best ones in the best locations. Location matters since a higher-end part of town might offer better quality clothing based on that demographic.

- Scrutinize items before purchasing and pay close attention to seams, buttons, and zippers. Look for quality fabrics that will withstand washing and inspect for stains.

- Consider wearing clothing that allows for easy try on— even in the middle of the store. Sometimes changing rooms are not available.

- Shop off-season for more discount opportunities—even in thrift stores.

- Be patient and persistent. Finding the best items may take some time. Visit regularly to browse new arrivals and increase your chance of finding treasures. Don't get discouraged if you don't see what you're looking for immediately. Keep searching, and you might be rewarded with great finds over time.

- Make it a date. Go with good friends who will be honest if your finds *fit* you and have fun catching up!

TAKING CARE OF THE CLOTHES YOU ALREADY HAVE

This is a quick explanation of how to take good care of the clothes you already have. As with anything in life, caring for your clothes properly from the beginning will postpone the need to replace them later, saving you time and money. Consider wearing an apron when cooking or doing outside work as a preventative measure.

The following are ten tips to help you extend the life of your clothing:

1. *Follow care labels.* Always read and follow the care instructions on clothing labels. Care instructions include washing, drying, and ironing guidelines. Proper care prevents damage and maintains the garment's original shape and color.

2. *Wash less frequently.* Avoid over-washing your clothes, as frequent washing can cause fabric wear and fading. Spot-clean when possible, and only wash garments when necessary to preserve quality.

3. *Use cold water.* Washing clothes in cold water can help prevent shrinkage and fading while saving energy. Cold water is gentle on fabrics and effective for cleaning most clothing items.

4. *Air dry when possible.* Air drying is gentler on clothes than drying them in a dryer, which can cause shrinkage and weaken fibers over time. Hang clothes on a drying rack or clothesline to maintain shape and texture.

5. *Invest in quality hangers.* Use sturdy hangers that support the shape of your clothes to prevent stretching and sagging. Padded or velvet hangers are ideal for delicate garments, while wooden hangers are great for heavier items like coats.

6. *Store properly.* Keep clothes in a cool, dry place away from direct sunlight to prevent fading and fabric damage. Use garment bags for delicate items, cedar blocks, or sachets to deter moths and other pests.

7. *Repair promptly.* Promptly address small issues like loose buttons, minor tears, or unraveling hems before they worsen. Learning basic sewing skills can help you make simple repairs at home, and this will save the day when something needs a quick repair while traveling.

8. *Rotate your wardrobe.* Regularly rotate your clothes to ensure even wear, which means not wearing the same items too frequently and giving them time to rest between wears.

9. *Use a bag when washing delicate clothing.* When washing delicate items, use a mesh laundry bag to protect them from snagging or getting stretched. It is handy for lingerie, knitwear, and items with embellishments.

10. *Don't overload the washer.* Overloading your washing machine can lead to poor cleaning and increased fabric wear and tear. Allow clothes to move freely in the wash for a more effective and gentle cleaning.

By following these tips, you can extend the life of your clothes and wardrobe, reducing the need for frequent replacements and saving money in the long run.

Being a frugal fashionista is all about embracing your style and confidence without feeling the pinch in your wallet. It's not about how much you spend but how you make it your own. So, get creative and find the best source for your own style. You may be surprised to learn that you don't need to spend a lot to look and feel fabulous.

11
HOME SWEET HOME OR SOMETHING SMALLER
NAVIGATING YOUR NEXT MOVE

"The home is the centerpiece of life. As we age,
it should evolve to support our changing needs,
while still reflecting who we are."

Martha Stewart

Does your home still work for you and your family efficiently? Will your current home meet your needs in the coming years? I'm referring to the long-term upkeep of your home, not only the day-to-day management. Kids grow and leave the nest, *most of the time*. As we age and the family dynamic shifts, we realize that our comfort and capabilities change, sometimes dramatically.

Is our home going to be too big? Too much to maintain? Too hard to maneuver through? Too much to heat or cool?

AGE IN PLACE OR DOWNSIZE

There are pros and cons to aging in place. Don and I chose our home because it had longevity, and we knew it could meet our changing needs while we lived out the rest of our lives. The floor plan worked well for our young family when we moved in 2001. We knew we could modify it to fit our family's needs as our family grew. Finally, we felt we could age in place as cute little old people.

Our home was a small cape-style house with one bedroom and one bathroom. The upstairs was an attic space converted into a room with a closet. Technically, it was a bedroom, but it was stuffy, hot in the summer, and cold in the winter. It was 1,000 square feet, and our boys had shared a downstairs bedroom for 17 years while we had the upstairs attic space. To call it tight would be an understatement.

After 17 years of living in a cramped space, my husband removed the roof of the house to add dormers. It's amazing! The man can do just about anything. The house went from just one room upstairs to two bedrooms, an office, and a bathroom. Talk about a dramatic improvement!

While it may sound perfect, the process took quite a bit of time and sacrifice before it was all said and done. In fact, it took my husband five years to complete this project, start to finish. During those five, long years, we moved our bed into the dining room. Yes, we slept in the dining room and ate at a super small table in the living room for FIVE YEARS! We saved our money, worked on the upstairs, and continued to save in order to pay for the renovation a little at a time. We essentially lived in 700 square feet with four people for five years, but now, it's perfect.

The original bedroom and bathroom remain downstairs, so when we're too old to climb a set of stairs, we will have everything we need on the bottom floor.

PROS OF AGING IN PLACE

One of the biggest perks of aging in place is staying in a familiar environment. You get to enjoy the comfort of the home you've built and loved over the years while maintaining independence and autonomy. There's something special about being surrounded by cherished memories and sentimental items that can boost your emotional well-being and give you a strong sense of security and stability.

Another great advantage is maintaining your community connections. Remaining in your original neighborhood allows you to keep social ties with neighbors, friends, and community members, fostering an essential sense of belonging and support which is critical to have in place as we age.

Plus, think of the cost savings! With the mortgage either paid off or soon to be, the main expense may just be property taxes. Often there are significant tax breaks for older adults. By staying put, you can avoid the moving costs, real estate fees, and renovation expenses of relocating. You also have the chance to customize your home with adaptable equipment, such as better lighting, grab bars, or ramps, to accommodate changing mobility needs and age-related challenges.

CONS TO AGING IN PLACE

On the flip side, there are some responsibilities to consider. Maintenance can become more demanding as the house gets older, which might be challenging for those on a fixed income. Safety concerns are also important, like making sure stairs, floors, and lighting don't pose any risks.

Social isolation is another potential issue if social connections diminish, or community support is limited. As I mentioned earlier, it's crucial to keep up those connections for physical and mental health.

PROS OF DOWNSIZING YOUR HOME

Downsizing opens the door to simplified living. Embracing a minimalistic lifestyle can be a massive benefit as you age. With fewer possessions and a smaller living space, you'll deal with less clutter and easier maintenance.

Financially, downsizing can be a win, too. You might reduce expenses like mortgage payments, property taxes, and utilities, freeing up funds for other priorities. Selling a larger home and paying cash for something smaller could also lead to financial freedom, especially if you use that money to clear out debt.

Downsizing offers greater flexibility and mobility, allowing you to explore new opportunities or travel without the burden of managing a large home. It's a chance to streamline your lifestyle, focusing on quality over quantity and prioritizing experiences and relationships over material possessions for a more fulfilling life.

CONS TO DOWNSIZING YOUR HOME

Downsizing does have its challenges, however. You might feel attached or nostalgic for your current home, making it tough to part with sentimental belongings or memories.

There's also the task of navigating the logistics of selling or relocating, which includes finding suitable housing, packing, and adjusting to a new environment. Adapting to a smaller space means downsizing belongings and dealing with limited storage.

Moving might also mean feeling disconnected from familiar surroundings and social networks, especially if you're moving to a new neighborhood with fewer connections. Of course, there are potential unknowns to consider, like changes in health or lifestyle that might impact your long-term housing needs.

Whether you age in place or decide to downsize, it's all about finding what works best for your lifestyle priorities, and budget.

12

THE COST OF COMFORT

MANAGING HOME EXPENSES WISELY

"Home is the nicest word there is."

Laura Ingalls Wilder

I am blessed with a brilliant husband who can repair or build almost anything. I know how blessed I am and that not everyone is as fortunate. This has saved us more money than I can even imagine. With that said, there are many things that anyone can do on their own, whether or not they choose to do the work is another story.

YouTube University has shared knowledge with the general public regarding just about anything. Obviously, YouTube University is not a real place—that's just what we call YouTube because of the information it holds. Whether you've decided to stay put or move to a smaller home, it is a given that you will encounter home-maintenance issues over time. Doing it yourself or DIYing, will save you a ton of money now.

However, there are some tasks that require a hired professional, such as anything related to electricity. I think it's a dangerous path to take without prior knowledge. However, preventative maintenance is something in which we can all take part.

REGULAR HVAC MAINTENANCE

Most people are capable of regular heating, ventilation, and air conditioning (HVAC) maintenance, which will help keep their systems running well. It's just a matter of knowing what to do and how often.

Change air filters every one to three months to ensure proper airflow and efficiency of your heating, ventilation, and HVAC system. Clean air vents and registers regularly to remove dust and debris, improving indoor air quality and HVAC performance. Insulate walls, floors, and attics to reduce heat loss in winter and heat gain in summer, improving overall energy efficiency.

CAULKING AND SEALING

Check your home for any gaps and cracks around windows, doors, and other openings where air and water can infiltrate your home. Even small gaps can be costly over time. Use caulking or weatherstripping to seal gaps and prevent drafts, improving energy efficiency and reducing heating and cooling costs. Inspect and replace worn or damaged seals around windows and doors to maintain a tight seal and prevent water intrusion, as well as air leaks.

Clean gutters and downspouts regularly to remove leaves, debris, and other obstructions that can cause water damage and flooding. Inspect gutters for signs of damage or rust and repair or replace damaged sections to ensure proper water drainage. Consider Installing gutter guards or screens to prevent debris buildup and minimize the need for frequent cleaning.

PLUMBING CHECKS

Inspect plumbing fixtures and pipes for leaks, drips, or signs of water damage. Repair or replace worn or leaking faucets, showerheads, and toilet flappers to conserve water and prevent costly water bills.

Check for signs of water damage or mold around sinks, toilets, and tubs, and address any underlying issues promptly. This is crucial for your health as well. Small leaks can create big issues if undetected that not only can be incredibly costly but also can cause many health issues.

ELECTRICAL SAFETY

Test smoke and carbon monoxide detectors regularly and replace batteries to ensure proper functionality. In parts of the country that practice daylight savings, the changing of the clocks is always a good reminder to change out batteries. If not, place a reminder in your phone or on a calendar.

Inspect electrical outlets, switches, and cords for signs of damage. Repair or replace them as necessary to prevent electrical hazards. Consider installing ground fault circuit interrupters (GFCIs) in kitchens, bathrooms, and outdoor areas to protect against electrical shocks and fires.

ENERGY TIPS TO REDUCE UTILITY BILLS

Energy bills are the biggest expense after food and housing. If we can find the sweet spot with the temperature, we can stretch ourselves a little bit and reduce it a smidge more. If you know that in hot temperatures, you are most comfortable when the air conditioning is set at 72 degrees, then bump it to 73 or 74 and see if it's still manageable. If it's 72 degrees and you're sitting on your lap with a blanket, watching YouTube, I would think you might have some wiggle room.

If you're a hot sleeper, feel free to reduce your bedroom temperature to Arctic sub-zero while you sleep with five blankets. There is no judgment there, but it will for sure impact your bill!

INSTALL ENERGY-EFFICIENT LIGHTING

Replace traditional incandescent bulbs with energy-efficient LED or CFL bulbs, which use significantly less energy and last longer.

Use motion sensor lights or timers to automatically turn off lights in unoccupied rooms and outdoor areas, reducing unnecessary energy consumption.

UPGRADE APPLIANCES

Invest in Energy Star-certified appliances, such as refrigerators, washing machines, and dishwashers, designed to be more energy efficient.

Consider replacing older appliances with newer models with advanced energy-saving features, such as eco-friendly wash cycles and smart technology.

PRACTICE ENERGY-SAVING HABITS

Turn off lights, electronics, and appliances when not in use to avoid phantom energy consumption. Use natural lighting and ventilation whenever possible by opening curtains and windows during daylight hours.

Wash clothes in cold water and air dry whenever feasible to reduce energy usage associated with hot water and dryer cycles.

Every frugal woman seeking to live a debt-free life should have a home maintenance plan. Entering retirement years or managing a tight budget shouldn't be an excuse for procrastinating on home maintenance. In fact, neglecting regular upkeep can end up costing you more in the long run.

To learn more about home maintenance tips, visit my website at frozenpennies.com.

13

RETAIL THERAPY REDEFINED

SPENDING WITH INTENT

"I like my money right where I can see it...
hanging in my closet."

Carrie Bradshaw
from Sex and the City

Unregulated emotions account for one of the biggest reasons many of us overspend. Maybe you go shopping every weekend because you *deserve* nice things. Possibly, you eat lunch out every day at work because you hate your job and need joy in your day, plus it's easier than making your lunch to bring. Your in-laws are driving you crazy so you go on an Amazon shopping spree. Whatever the reason, emotions often are a factor. We could take this even further and say it's the reason for the "too much" house or bougie car—we want people to tell us how nice our things are, which makes us feel good about ourselves.

I can honestly admit that I am an imperfect, flawed woman. Even though I am frugal, I've been known to spend a good bit of money when I knew better not to. Shopping trips to BJ's Warehouse (for my non-New Yorker audience, it's like Costco for Upstate N.Y.) can create a deficit in my personal profit and loss statement. If there were a Costco near me, it would be a double deficit in my account, I'm positive!

What does it say about me that I would rather spend $300 at BJ's than on a Michael Kors purse? My husband would say it's because I'm practical.

LEARN HOW TO MANAGE EMOTIONS

I feel a little bad about telling a midlife woman who could very well be starting her journey into perimenopause to learn to manage emotions. I apologize ahead of time. Learn to identify these triggers. The key to change is recognizing the emotions or situations that trigger overspending, such as stress, boredom, or social pressure. Keep a journal to track your spending with a notation of the emotions or circumstances surrounding the purchases which may help identify patterns and triggers that could lead to overspending.

Practice mindfulness when spending money. Cultivate awareness and mindfulness techniques to tune in with your thoughts, emotions, and impulses in the moment. Pause, take a deep breath, and count to 10 before making impulse purchases. This solid pause gives you time to assess whether the purchase aligns with your financial goals and values.

Set clear, established boundaries and limits for your spending by creating a budget and sticking to it. Stay committed to returning to the budget no matter how often you feel like you failed. Giving up is not an option; we all mess up the budget. We continue to go back to it. Determine discretionary spending allowances for non-essential purchases and avoid exceeding these at all costs to prevent overspending. Develop coping strategies other than overspending. Building healthy coping strategies to manage your emotions without resorting to retail therapy or impulsive shopping will still give you that feel-good feeling without imploding your financial goals. Engage in alternative activities that provide emotional fulfillment and stress relief, such as exercise, hobbies, doing something nice for someone, or self-care. Surround yourself with a supportive network of friends, family, and a counselor who can offer encouragement, accountability, and guidance in managing spending habits. Seek their support if you feel totally out of control. Consider a support group or online community focused on financial wellness and overcoming overspending. This way, you can share experiences and learn from others.

Set up a budget for those areas and identify problem areas. What are the places where you most likely overspend? Begin by identifying specific categories or items that regularly mess up your budget. Areas of overspending could include dining out, clothing, entertainment, or hobbies. Review past spending habits to analyze where most of your discretionary spending goes and how to set realistic guidelines for yourself and your spending.

Allocate a realistic allowance for each problem area based on your income and money goals. When setting up these allowances, consider all factors, such as the overall budget, essential expenses, savings goals, and debt repayment obligations. Use cash envelopes or digital tools to take you to the next level.

Consider using the cash envelope system, where you allocate physical cash into envelopes labeled with each problem area's budget, as I mentioned earlier in the book. Alternatively, use digital budgeting tools or apps to set spending limits for specific categories and track your expenses in real-time. Track and monitor your spending within each allocated budget category regularly to ensure you stay within your limits. Review your expenses weekly in the beginning, then monthly later to assess your progress and identify any areas where adjustments may be necessary. Adjust as needed and be flexible and willing to adjust your budget allocations as required based on changes in income, expenses, or priorities. If you consistently overspend in certain areas despite setting allowances, reassess your budget and consider reallocating funds from other categories or finding alternative strategies to control spending.

BE INTENTIONAL

Be the boss of your money through intentional spending. Take time to clarify your short-term and long-term financial goals, whether paying off debt, saving for a vacation, or building an emergency fund. Having clear goals gives you a sense of purpose and motivation to be intentional with your spending. Visualize your financial goals by creating a vision board or using visual aids to represent your aspirations.

Display your vision board in a prominent place where you'll see it daily as a reminder of what you're working towards. Acknowledge and celebrate your progress towards your financial goals, no matter how small. Recognize and celebrate milestones to help keep you motivated and reinforce positive financial habits. Cultivate gratitude for what you already have and your progress on your financial journey. Focus on appreciating the value and purpose of your purchases rather than seeking instant gratification through material possessions. Stay positive and maintain a growth mindset, viewing challenges as opportunities for learning and growth. Be persistent and intentional with your spending, knowing that every small step brings you closer to financial empowerment and freedom.

GIFT GIVING

As we age, our need for physical things becomes less exciting. I know that many frown upon giving money or gift cards, but as adults, I think it's the best! It certainly works for us.

Our oldest son and daughter-in-law would rather have cash or gift cards than gifts just to get a gift. They are a young family in that season of life, and a Target gift card can be used for diapers, groceries, or new socks, whatever my daughter-in-law wants or needs, it's her choice. The gift still means the same.

If someone were to give me a Starbucks gift card, I would be giddy with excitement! Yes, I can buy my own cup of coffee, but the idea that someone knows me well enough to know what I love is more of a gift and always appreciated. It is very important to me to be intentional about giving. I tend to listen to people and store up ideas for later.

As an example, at my daughter-in-law's third baby shower, which her friends called a *mist* she received a bag of Lindt chocolates. She was excited about it and mentioned that the key lime pie and coconut flavors were her favorites. So, for Christmas, I will do my darndest to see if I can find those flavors. By the way, her friends considered the first baby celebration as a traditional shower, the second baby was a *sprinkle*, and the third baby was a *mist*. *So cute, right?*

If you have a lot of people to buy for, especially children, consider collecting Christmas gifts all year long. Look for clearance items and new or like-new items at thrift stores or garage sales.

Unregulated emotions often lead to impulse buys that leave us feeling regretful. By redefining retail therapy and spending with intent, you're taking back control of your choices and your wallet. Remember, it's not about avoiding spending entirely but making sure it aligns with your values and goals. You deserve to feel good about the way you spend.

For more resources on this, check out <u>frozenpennies.com/fun.</u>

14

FROM CRADLE TO COLLEGE

FINANCIAL STRATEGIES FOR EVERY STAGE OF PARENTHOOD

"Being a mom has made me so tired. And so happy."

Tina Fey

Children need a place in this *Fundamentally Frugal* book for sure. Although my children are fully grown, I have friends who still have children at home. In fact, one friend in her 40s has a precious five-year-old daughter who's the same age as my oldest granddaughter.

Whether you have grown children, young children, or kids someplace in the middle, most of us can relate to the cost of children at home. Raising kids is one of life's most rewarding adventures, but let's be real—it can also be quite the financial challenge! Every stage of your child's life, from diapers to college tuition, presents unique opportunities to save money without sacrificing quality or fun. Let's explore some friendly tips and tricks for each age group to help you keep more money in your wallet while providing the best for your children.

BABY AND TODDLER YEARS

Ah, the baby and toddler years—filled with cuddles, giggles, and many unplanned expenses! Don't worry, I'll share plenty of ways to save during this precious time. First, as a new parent, consider buying second-hand clothes and gear. Babies grow at lightning speed, and gently used clothes, toys, and furniture can save you a bundle. You'll find many items in excellent condition at consignment shops, online marketplaces, or even from friends and family.

Next, if you choose to use formula, look for store brands or buy in bulk. Store brands often meet the same nutritional standards as name brands and are significantly cheaper. Don't forget to sign up for coupons and samples from formula companies—they can be lifesavers! Of course, if you're able to breastfeed, it is the best option to provide natural nutrition to your baby, and just happens to be an excellent way to save money.

Making your own baby food is another fantastic way to save money and ensure your little one is getting wholesome, clean nutrition. It's easier than you might think—just steam, blend, and freeze fruits and veggies in ice cube trays for easy portioning. You can make large batches and store them in the freezer, saving time during hectic days.

Consider borrowing or swapping toys and books with other parents. Babies and toddlers are fascinated by new things, and swapping with friends is a fun way to keep things fresh without constantly buying new toys. Libraries are also a treasure trove for borrowing books, offering variety without the cost.

The needs and expenses of daycare also should be addressed. In an age where single parents and dual incomes are more prevalent than stay-at-home parents, daycare is often needed and can be expensive. Therefore, it needs to be prominently accounted for in the budget.

My oldest son and daughter-in-law send their three children to daycare. She could probably afford to stay home, but she loves her job and loves the life it affords them. We live in a country where women get to decide what they want to do if they make good money.

Sometimes it's about more than just financial security. It's about having the option to live in a way that aligns with who you are. For some women, staying at home and raising children feels right. For others, like my daughter-in-law, a career is a source of pride and accomplishment. It's empowering to live in a time when women aren't forced into a role, and they can thrive in professional and family lives if they choose to do so.

However, often, the choice is made through necessity to be able to afford basic things, such as a roof over their head and food on their table.

Daycare comes at a cost, both literally and figuratively.

Other options might be having a family member who's willing to help out, daycare centers versus private in-home centers, or hiring a nanny in your home. If you have children and need or want to work, this is something that needs serious thought and conversations.

Finally, keep your baby and toddler gear simple and practical. It's easy to get caught up in the excitement of buying all the latest gadgets and products, but most aren't necessary. Focus on essentials and items that will grow with your child, like convertible car seats and cribs that transform into toddler beds. By choosing multipurpose products, you save money and space.

SCHOOL AGE YEARS

Once your child reaches school age, expenses shift to include education, activities, and social events. One great tip for saving money during these years is to buy school supplies in bulk. Stock up on essentials like pencils, notebooks, and crayons during back-to-school sales, and keep an inventory at home so you're not caught off guard mid-year.

Next, encourage your kids to be involved in low-cost or free extracurricular activities, such as community sports leagues or clubs at school. These activities can provide great socialization and learning experiences without breaking the bank. Many community centers and libraries offer free or low-cost programs and classes, ranging from sports to arts and crafts, that can be perfect for school-age children.

Another smart strategy is to pack lunches. It is typically cheaper than buying school lunches and allows you to ensure your kids are eating healthy, well-balanced meals. With the rise in food allergies among our kids, this also ensures their safety. Get your kids involved in planning and preparing their lunches to make it a fun, collaborative experience. Packing lunches saves money and teaches them valuable skills in nutrition and budgeting.

When it comes to clothing, consider buying off-season. Stores often sell winter clothes at the end of the season or summer clothes as fall approaches. Take advantage of these sales to buy the next size up for your kids at a fraction of the cost. Hand-me-downs are also great, especially if you have more than one child or can swap with friends and family.

Lastly, consider organizing or participating in a toy and book exchange with other parents. Kids can quickly lose interest in their toys and exchanging them can be a cost-effective way to keep them entertained and engaged with new items without purchasing them. It's a win-win for everyone involved!

TEEN YEARS

Ah, the teenage years! They come with unique challenges and expenses, but you can keep costs manageable with creativity. Start by teaching your teens about budgeting and financial responsibility. Please encourage them to earn their own money through part-time jobs, helping neighbors, or with chores around the house. Earning their own money helps them contribute to their own expenses and teaches them valuable life skills about earning and saving money. Clothing and trends can be significant expenses during the teenage years. Encourage your teens to embrace thrift shopping. Many teens enjoy the thrill of finding unique clothing items at thrift stores, and it can be a great way to save money on their wardrobe. You also can encourage them to host clothing swap parties with friends, where they can trade gently used clothes they no longer wear. This is especially helpful for girls attending school dances!

For those who drive, consider helping them find a fuel-efficient vehicle or suggest they use public transportation, bike, or carpool whenever possible to save on gas and reduce environmental impact. Additionally, involving them in researching and comparing auto insurance rates can teach them the importance of getting the best deal. In some situations, the teen could pay the increase in insurance to drive. Knowing that an accident or a citation could increase their financial responsibility may make them more conscientious drivers.

Regarding ever changing technology, encourage teens to care for their devices to avoid costly repairs or replacements. Discuss the option of buying refurbished gadgets, which can be significantly cheaper than brand-new ones and often come with warranties. Make them responsible financially for repairing devices and quickly they become even more careful.

Finally, encourage your teens to explore free- or low-cost entertainment options, such as community events, outdoor activities, or family streaming services for movies and music. Teaching them to find joy in simple, affordable activities can help them develop a frugal mindset that lasts a lifetime.

COLLEGE YEARS

Before I start with the college years, I want you to join me for a cup of coffee out on the deck. I want you to be open-minded when I say this...

If you are not regularly contributing to your retirement fund and are drowning in consumer debt, you should NOT be saving for your child's college education.

I know. I may just lose you right here. We feel, as parents, that it's our duty to pay this very large sum of money and contribute to the success of our children's future. I hear you and acknowledge the good in your heart.

However, if they genuinely want to attend college, and you are not in a position to pay for it, your sweet baby will figure it all out. Not only will they find a way, they also will thrive because they are fully financially committed.

Let me tell you a story about my son's friend, John. John is an impressive young man. He worked his way through community college by holding a job and saving for a semester or two at a time. He paid his tuition with cash. When, he no longer had tuition money, he took off for a summer and/or a semester to work full-time in order to earn enough money for his next two or more semesters. It took him much longer to earn that degree, but he found a way to make it happen. I'm super proud of him and know that his diligence will pay off greatly for him in the future.

We raised our youngest to understand that not only had we been unable to save for his college education, but we were also not signing any papers for him to take out student loans. So, if college was in his heart, then he needed to do well enough to get scholarships or work while in school. He also knew that when the time came, we would help as much as we could, but he had to make it happen.

Make it happen, he did! New York has a great program called the Excelsior Scholarship, which allows families within a specific income bracket to attend a state school on scholarship, with guidelines and rules of course. So, that's what he did.

Understanding that when you are in your 40s, you have a much shorter time to invest in your elder years than your child has to figure out what they want to do with their lives and invest in further education.

This philosophy does not mean that you love your child any less. It means that there's a chance they will be a better student, likely with more studying and less partying, if they are or have paid for it themselves. Whether through scholarships, grants, or just hard work, they will find a way.

The college years are notoriously expensive, but there are still many ways to save. First, encourage your college-bound kids to apply for scholarships and grants, always. There are countless opportunities available, and every bit of financial aid can help reduce the burden of tuition and fees.

Consider having your child attend a community college for the first two years. State community colleges can drastically reduce the cost of a degree while allowing them to complete general education requirements before transferring to a four-year university.

Another money-saving tip is to buy or rent textbooks online. Textbooks can be a significant expense, so purchasing used copies or renting them from online platforms can save substantial money. Please encourage your child to sell their textbooks at the end of each semester to recoup some of the costs. If your student is not responsible for tuition, consider making them responsible for purchasing their own books. It's remarkable how creative they get when it's their own money!

Help your college student learn to budget and manage their money. Please encourage them to use apps or tools that track spending and discuss the importance of sticking to a budget.

Consider opening a student checking account with no fees to help them manage their finances more effectively.

Encourage your college students to take advantage of campus resources and discounts. Many colleges offer free or discounted access to events, fitness facilities, and transportation. These resources can save students money and enhance their college experience.

ADULT CHILDREN

Even when your children are grown, there are still ways to help them save money and allow you to support their financial independence. One great tip is to encourage them to live at home temporarily while they save for their own place. This arrangement can be mutually beneficial, allowing them to save on rent while contributing to household expenses and/or helping with chores.

Encourage your adult children to create and stick to a budget, focusing on paying down student loans or debt. Discuss the importance of emergency savings and help them set up an account to build a financial safety net. This is critical.

Consider gifting them experiences rather than material items for birthdays and holidays. Experiences, like travel or classes, can be more meaningful and memorable, and they often contribute to personal growth and happiness without cluttering up their space.

If they move out for the first time, suggest buying gently used furniture and household items. Thrift stores, online marketplaces, and garage sales can offer great deals on quality items, helping them furnish their space affordably.

Lastly, continue to model good financial habits and have open discussions about money. Share your experiences and encourage them to ask questions, as well as to seek advice when needed. Being a financial mentor can help them make informed decisions and develop a strong foundation for their financial future.

Raising kids involves many expenses, but applying these tips at every stage of your child's life can save money while supporting their growth and happiness. Whether it's through teaching them financial responsibility or finding creative ways to cut costs, you'll be setting them up for a financially secure future. Plus, you'll create a family culture that values frugality and mindfulness, benefiting everyone in the long run.

15

RETIRE WITH EASE

DITCHING DEBT WITHOUT FEELING THE SQUEEZE

"Balancing your money is the key to having enough."

Elizabeth Warren

If you can only get one thing out of this book, please let it be this: *It's so very important to pay off all your debt and vow NEVER to return.*

This is a big chapter full of great tips, but most importantly, your mental and emotional well-being will shift significantly once your debt, including your home mortgage, has been paid off. There's no greater feeling in your financial journey than to be completely debt-free.

On one of those trips from the library with my arms full of books about money, I came across a book called *The Total Money*

Makeover by Dave Ramsey. Little did I know that this book would literally change my life and open so many new doors for me.

Let's start at the beginning. We had just straightened out our foreclosure issues by refinancing our home with the same bank, and we were safe from the terror of being homeless.

I swore that I would do better.

In *The Total Money Makeover*, Dave taught me a few things. My biggest takeaway from the book was the gift of control over our money and a plan for our future. It was like somebody had just turned on a light. Not only did I learn what a budget was (I had an idea), but I also learned how to implement that budget. Most importantly, I learned how to follow through with that budget every day without fail. My idea regarding cash envelopes for things like Christmas, groceries, clothes, haircuts, and pet food, came from his book. I gained confidence that when we needed groceries, we already had the money in the envelope.

Through Dave's book I gained the vision to look ahead and realize that not only could we pay off our house much sooner than the 30-year mortgage, but we also could work toward becoming completely debt-free. After much hard work and dedication, we achieved our goal to become debt-free. We paid off more than $70,000 in debt, including our house in seven years, paying off our house 15 years earlier than anticipated, and we have never looked back. To this day, we have zero debt.

Before we go on, I want to talk about credit cards for a hot second.

We may have had it easier when it came to getting out of debt because we didn't have credit cards. It's not because we didn't want them—it's because the banks wouldn't approve us to receive them.

You see, we had both gotten into a hole with credit cards. Mine started straight out of high school. JCPenney had a table set up outside their store, giving away candy bars. All I needed to do was fill out an application for a credit card to receive the chocolate, so I did. I mean it was *chocolate,* and I had no willpower. Even without a job, they granted me a $350 credit limit. Who gives a jobless 18-year-old a credit card with $350 to spend? JCPenney did!

That was the start of my credit card debt drama. I then was approved for a Discover Card, as well as another clothing store card. I went away to college with a kick-butt new wardrobe and zero comprehensiveness as to how I would ever pay back the almost $1,000 debt, not including the interest that built up quickly. I had no clue how that was going to happen.

Once I paid off the collectors the following summer, my credit was shot, and I was terrified of credit cards. It took me 30 years before I had another.

After Don's divorce, he vowed NEVER to have another credit card again, spoken from a place of anger, pain, and doubt. He'd been over-extended and had more than $30,000 in consumer debt when his marriage ended. He had been burned and burned bad.

Those were solid lessons to learn in the early years of our marriage, as they made becoming debt-free a smidge easier. In the last five years, we have chosen bravery and now have a couple of credit cards that get paid off monthly, as a firm rule.

It took me a long time to apply for a credit card again. For many years, I knew myself well enough to recognize that I was not disciplined enough to control my usage. Even today, I understand that people spend more with plastic than with cash.

I owe that to *The Total Money Makeover*—so much so that I joined Dave Ramsey's team and became a Financial Coach in 2019.

Even though I don't follow every rule that Dave stands firmly behind and am not 100 percent on board with his philosophies, I have meshed together some of his smart teachings with lessons learned through the years to come up with my own coaching style. It all started with that money book borrowed from the library all those years ago.

WHY IT'S IMPORTANT

Financial freedom is a glorious feeling! Eliminating debt reduces financial obligations, providing flexibility and peace of mind in retirement. It also reduces monthly expenses dramatically. Without those monthly payments and interest, you free up more money for essential living expenses and fun. Paying everything off reduces financial vulnerability and protects retirement savings from unforeseen events or economic downturns. It simply reduces overall risk. Without debt obligations, you have more discretionary income for savings, investment, travel, or hobbies. Owning your home fully not only provides a valuable asset and safeguards your financial security in retirement but also gives you a sense of peace nobody can take away. You will always have a place to live, as long as you continue to pay your property taxes.

HOW TO PAY OFF DEBTS

The two most popular methods of paying off debts are the debt snowball and the debt avalanche. I prefer the snowball method because I like quick wins, but both are effective, depending on your personality and values.

When it comes to paying off debt, there are two popular methods that people tend to use: the debt snowball and the debt avalanche. Personally, I'm a big fan of the debt snowball because I love those quick wins—they really keep you motivated! But honestly, both methods work well; it just depends on your personality and what you value more.

With the debt snowball, here's what you do:

First, list all your debts, including the balances, interest rates, and minimum payments. Then, arrange them from the smallest to the largest balance, ignoring the interest rates for now. You'll make the minimum payments on everything except the smallest debt, and that's where the magic happens. Any extra money you have goes toward paying off that smallest debt as fast as possible. Once that debt is knocked out, you roll over what you were paying on it to the next smallest debt. It's like building momentum—a snowball effect—until eventually, you're debt-free. The best part? You get to celebrate each debt you pay off, which keeps that motivation going strong. With every debt you eliminate, your payments get bigger and bigger as you redirect those amounts to the next one on your list. There's something fantastic about crossing off those debts one by one while you work your way down.

Now, if you're more focused on minimizing the amount of interest you pay, the debt avalanche might be more your style. In this method, you'll start by listing all your debts, just like before, but this time you'll arrange them by interest rate, from highest to lowest. Make the minimum payments on everything, except the debt with the highest interest rate. Put any extra funds toward aggressively paying that one off. Once that's done, roll over what you were paying on it to the next debt with the highest interest rate. You'll keep going until you're debt-free, gaining momentum like an avalanche, all while focusing on saving money on interest. Of course, don't forget to celebrate along the way!

So, whether you like the quick wins of the snowball method or prefer the long-term savings of the avalanche, the key is sticking with whichever approach feels best for you and fits your personality. Either way, you're working toward the same goal— being debt-free!

SHOULD YOU USE YOUR SAVINGS TO ELIMINATE YOUR DEBTS?

The short answer is, "it depends."

Here are my tips for using savings to pay off debt. First and foremost, it's important to assess your financial situation. Take a step back and look at the bigger picture, including the total amount of debt you have, the interest rates on those debts, and your current savings and retirement goals. Before making any decisions, also consider factors like job stability, your health, and any other financial obligations that might pop up.

Once you've done that, it's time to develop a plan. You want to create a realistic repayment plan that balances paying off debt, with keeping a solid emergency fund and continuing to save for retirement. If you think that your debt can be paid off quickly and you have a few thousand dollars in a starter emergency fund, I say go ahead and pause everything else then throw every single penny you can scrounge up and knock out that debt super fast.

Set specific goals and timelines for paying off your debt, and make sure to track your progress along the way. This way, you can stay on track and make adjustments as needed. Plus, tracking your progress is always fun—make it a game!

Now, let's talk about the advantages of using your savings to pay off debt. First, it can provide some immediate relief from those high-interest payments, which can really reduce financial stress. Once those debts are gone, you'll be able to add any of that extra money toward retirement, helping you hit those long-term goals faster. Plus, being debt-free brings so much peace of mind and gives you more financial freedom, especially as you head into retirement. By paying off high-interest debts with savings, you can also save money in the long run by avoiding interest, which might be a better move than keeping that money in a savings account earning just a few cents a month.

However, there are also some disadvantages. Using your savings to pay off debt means you're dipping into your emergency fund, which could leave you vulnerable if unexpected expenses arise. If your savings are down to *nothing* and an emergency happens, you might find yourself relying on credit cards or loans again. Depending on where your savings are held—like in retirement or taxable investment accounts—there could be tax implications when you withdraw the funds to pay off debt.

So, before making any big moves, weigh the pros and cons to see if using your savings to pay off debt is the right choice for you.

SHOULD YOU USE RETIREMENT SAVINGS TO PAY OFF DEBTS?

As a financial coach, I strongly urge anyone to use their retirement savings as a last resort. If you cannot eliminate all consumer debt and your mortgage before you retire, then using your retirement savings might need to be your answer. However, there are pros and cons to this, too. You'll have to determine the right answer for you, but the following are some additional points to consider.

When it comes to using retirement funds to pay off debt, there are a few key things to keep in mind. First, it's super important to learn what the tax implications might be if you take money out of your retirement early. Depending on your situation, there may be penalties and taxes to consider. It's always a good idea to consult with a tax advisor or financial planner to understand how this decision could impact your overall financial position.

You'll want to carefully weigh the long-term implications of using retirement savings versus exploring other debt payoff options. If, after thinking long and hard about this, using your retirement funds seems like the best route, it's important to create a repayment plan that won't destroy your future retirement plans. Make sure you set specific goals and timelines for repaying or saving to replace those funds, and track your progress regularly to stay on top of your retirement goals.

There are some advantages to using retirement funds to pay off debt. First, it can provide immediate relief from high-interest payments, which reduces financial stress. By eliminating your debt, you free up future income to go towards savings and investments for retirement.

Paying off high-interest debt with retirement funds can also save you money in the long run by reducing the amount of interest you'll pay over time. This can even potentially outweigh the money you would have earned on those retirement investments. It also makes your financial situation simpler, reducing the risk of carrying debt into retirement and giving you a clean slate to focus on building up your savings for the future.

However, there are also some disadvantages of which to be aware. Withdrawing retirement funds before reaching retirement age often comes with early withdrawal penalties and taxes, which can significantly impact your savings and the effects of compound interest. Cashing in those funds means sacrificing the potential for growth, which could have helped your retirement savings grow over time. This can also delay or mess up your retirement goals, making it harder to achieve the retirement lifestyle of which you've dreamed. So, while using retirement funds to pay off debt can bring immediate relief, it's important to thoroughly evaluate the long-term impact on your financial future.

In the end, the decision to use retirement funds to pay off debt should be made carefully, fully understanding of the trade-offs.

This is definitely a time to speak with both a tax professional and a financial advisor. Do not take borrowing from your retirement savings lightly.

IS THERE GOOD DEBT?

Phew...Nope.

Many people disagree with me on this, and that's okay, but keep reading, and allow me to expand upon this and explain my thoughts.

Some feel that owning a home is good debt. You get a tax write-off on the interest that you pay every month. In the grand scheme of things, that is not a lot of benefit, and I do not feel like it is enough benefit to hold on to your home. Having a mortgage is okay. It's acceptable but far from good.

We have two rental properties that we purchased with cash. I understand that it's a rare occurrence that a person can find a solid rental property for $50,000, pay cash, invest another $10,000, and rent it out for $1,500 a month. So, if you can't do that and want to invest in rental properties, taking a loan out is an option. I still don't believe that is *good* debt, but it's not terrible. There needs to be plenty of padding put into place if this is something that you plan on doing. Remember, if you're renting the property out for the same amount that the mortgage is and something happens, where will that payment come from for the months that the property is empty.

Do you have an emergency fund to pay the mortgage? What if the roof needs a repair or the basement gets flooded? Are you financially prepared for these things without taking out more money, putting it on a credit card, or robbing your personal funds to cover those expenses?

I had someone reach out to me and tell me they borrowed against their retirement account to buy a property so their daughter could live there with two roommates. This means that as rent came in, it could go toward paying off that retirement account loan, and so they were paying themselves back with interest.

I am highly risk averse. The thought of borrowing money knowing that the minute we lose that job, we must immediately pay it back, or the tax penalties are outrageous. The risk does not outweigh the benefits. We took money out of my husband's retirement account after he retired to buy a second rental property, and the taxes on that were super painful to pay.

If you have a loan on a rental property, like a mortgage, it's *okay* debt. It's *more* okay if your residence is paid off.

Paying off all your debt isn't just a financial move—it's a promise to yourself for a stress-free retirement. It's about ditching the burden and never looking back. By making that commitment, you're setting yourself up to enjoy the freedom and peace for which you've worked so hard.

16
READY. SET. RETIRE.

TIMING YOUR GOLDEN EXIT

"Retirement isn't the end of the road; it's the
beginning of the open highway."

Jane Fonda

Deciding when to retire is a significant life decision, and as a midlife woman, there are many factors to consider ensuring you make the best choice for yourself and your family. Let's review several critical aspects to consider, helping you confidently navigate this exciting transition.

FINANCIAL PREPAREDNESS

First, let's discuss finances. Ask yourself, "Are my investments in good enough shape to support my retirement lifestyle?" Take a close look at your savings in your 401(k), IRAs, and other investment accounts. Calculate your expected expenses and compare them with your projected income to ensure you can live comfortably without financial stress.

Another key consideration are Social Security benefits. While you can begin accessing your Social Security benefits at age 62, each year you are able to wait to collect will significantly boost your monthly amount until age 67. It's worth weighing the pros and cons of taking benefits early versus waiting for a bigger payout. If you have other income sources and can afford to delay, you might find it beneficial to wait and maximize your benefits.

Keep track of any pensions or annuities you might have. If you're lucky enough to have a pension plan, understand how it fits into your financial picture. Knowing when and how to access these funds is crucial for retirement planning.

Managing debt is another biggie. Entering retirement with high levels of debts can strain your finances, so aim to pay off any high-interest debts like credit cards or loans before you retire. Complete freedom from debt frees up more of your income for the fun and relaxation you've earned after decades of hard work. I just shared a few good tips with how to do this in the previous chapter.

Let's not overlook an emergency savings account. A solid emergency fund can help cover unexpected expenses like medical bills or home repairs, ensuring you don't have to dip into your retirement savings prematurely. Saving up at least three to six months of living expenses is best, more if at all possible.

HEALTH AND WELL-BEING

The state of your health is a huge factor in deciding when to retire. Consider your health and how it might change in the coming years. If you have health issues requiring more rest or medical care, retiring earlier could be beneficial. For some with health issues early in life, they are forced to retire sooner than they had planned. However, if you're in good health and enjoy your work, you might choose to work longer and keep building your savings.

Think about your health insurance coverage as well. If you retire before age 65, you won't be eligible for Medicare yet, so you must plan for interim health coverage. Health insurance can be a significant expense, so exploring your options is important, whether through a spouse's plan, COBRA, or private insurance. Also, consider that there will still be expenses even with Medicare. It does not cover 100 percent of medical expenses, so factor that into your planning.

Mental and emotional well-being is just as important as physical health. Consider your level of job satisfaction. Continuing to work might be appealing if you find your work fulfilling and enjoy the social interaction it provides. On the other hand, if your job is a source of stress or dissatisfaction, retiring sooner could improve your quality of life.

FAMILY AND SOCIAL DYNAMICS

Your family and social dynamics can significantly influence your decision to retire. If you're married or have a partner, it is essential to discuss your retirement plans to ensure you're both on the same page. Consider your partner's health and retirement plans, as these factors will affect your decision and financial planning.

If you have aging parents, think about their health and potential needs for caregiving. Are you prepared to support them physically and/or financially? How might that impact your retirement timeline? Additionally, consider the possibility of becoming a caregiver for grandchildren. If providing childcare for your grandkids is something you would consider, factor that possibility into your retirement plans.

Your social connections are another important consideration. Retirement often means leaving behind a work community, so thinking about how to stay socially active is essential. Engaging in volunteer work, joining clubs/social groups, or taking classes can help maintain your social life and give you a sense of purpose.

LIFESTYLE AND PERSONAL GOALS

Think about what you want your retirement to look like. Do you have personal goals or dreams you'd like to pursue? Whether traveling, starting a new hobby, or spending more time with family, consider how retirement can help you achieve these goals.

Consider the cost of your desired lifestyle. Are you planning to travel extensively, or are you content with a more modest lifestyle close to home? Your lifestyle choices will significantly impact how much money you need in retirement, so it's important to align your financial plan with your goals.

As we discussed in an earlier chapter, *but worth reemphasizing*, housing decisions are also crucial. Do you plan to stay in your current home? Are you considering downsizing or relocating? Each option has financial implications, so consider the costs of moving, maintaining your home, or adjusting to a new location. Downsizing can free up equity and reduce expenses while staying put, which might offer emotional comfort and stability.

TIMING AND FLEXIBILITY

Retirement doesn't have to be an all-or-nothing decision. Consider phased retirement or part-time work as an option. Gradually reducing your work hours can provide a transition period, allowing you to adjust to retirement life while still earning an income. This approach can help ease the financial and emotional transition into full retirement. Depending on your experience, another option could be freelance work or as a substitute employee with a business in your area of expertise. Economic factors and market conditions can also influence your timing. If the economy is unstable or your investments are underperforming, you might work a little longer to allow your portfolio to recover. Staying flexible and adaptable is key to making a successful transition to retirement.

Finally, consider the impact of retirement on your identity and purpose. Many people find that work provides a sense of identity and purpose. Reflect on how you'll maintain a sense of purpose and fulfillment in retirement through volunteering, hobbies, or new ventures.

Deciding when to retire is a deeply personal decision that involves weighing various financial, health, family, and lifestyle factors. By considering these aspects and having open discussions with your family and financial advisor, can help you create a retirement plan that aligns with your and your family's goals and values. Remember, there's no one-size-fits-all answer, and it's essential to do what feels right for you and your circumstances. Retirement is a new chapter in life, allowing you to explore new interests, enjoy more time with loved ones, and live according to your schedule. With careful planning and consideration, you can make the most of this exciting transition and embrace retirement's possibilities.

17

COVERAGE AND GROWTH

SIMPLIFYING INSURANCE AND INVESTMENTS IN MIDLIFE

"Real change, enduring change, happens one step
at a time."

Ruth Bader Ginsburg

Before we start, this is a general overview of some common investment strategies and insurance you might encounter. I am not a financial advisor, and I cannot, in good conscience, advise you on whether or not these will work for you. If you think any of these *could* work for you and *would* like to know more information, consider setting up an appointment with a financial advisor in your area. It is never a bad idea to consult with a licensed financial advisor and always better to have a base-level of knowledge prior to meeting with a professional.

DISCLAIMER:

This information is for informational purposes only. I am not a financial advisor. I am a Ramsey Solutions Financial Coach, but I am not your financial coach. This chapter is intended as thought and conversation starters that should be discussed with a certified financial advisor.

Let's explore some broad investment strategies, including various retirement accounts, and delve into different types of insurance to help you make informed decisions for your financial future. Understanding these options can empower you to plan effectively and secure your financial well-being.

RETIREMENT INVESTMENT STRATEGIES

Planning for retirement is one of the most important financial goals you can set, and there are several ways to build a nest egg that will support you in your golden years. Let's start with some of the most common retirement investment options. These plans will have the greatest impact if they are implemented as soon as you start full-time work.

401(K)

Many employers offer a 401(k) retirement savings plan. It's like a unique piggy bank for your future. You can direct money from your paycheck into this account before taxes are taken out, which means you save money on taxes in the present. The best part? Many employers will match a portion of what you save, which is like getting free money for your retirement! This is why you should max out your contribution, so you don't leave money on the table.

403(B)

A 403(b) is similar to a 401(k), but it's specifically designed for employees of non-profit organizations, like schools and hospitals. It helps you save for retirement by allowing you to contribute part of your salary before taxes are taken out. Just like with a 401(k), you might receive matching contributions from your employer, significantly boosting your savings.

INDIVIDUAL RETIREMENT ACCOUNTS (IRA)

A Roth IRA is a retirement savings account funded by you with earnings already taxed. However, the cool thing about a Roth IRA is that in retirement, you can withdraw your money tax-free. It's a great way to save for the future if you think you'll be in a higher tax bracket when you retire. Plus, it gives you a lot of flexibility and control over your investments.

Keep in mind, there is an income limit to make a full contribution. According to the Fidelity website, "The IRS restricts who can contribute based on modified adjusted gross income (MAGI)...The Roth IRA income limit to make a full contribution in 2024 is less than $146,000 for single filers, and less than $230,000 for those filing jointly. If you're a single filer, you're eligible to contribute a portion of the full amount if your MAGI is $146,000 or more, but less than $161,000." https://www.fidelity.com/learning-center/smart-money/roth-ira-income-limits

TRADITIONAL IRA

A traditional IRA is another type of retirement savings account. You can contribute money to this account with a tax break in the year you contribute. Your money grows tax-deferred, meaning you only pay taxes once you withdraw it once in retirement. A traditional IRA can be a smart option if you want to lower your taxable income now and expect a lower tax bracket later.

INDEX FUNDS

Index funds are like a big basket of different stocks or bonds. When you invest in an index fund, you buy a small piece of all the companies in a specific index, like the S&P 500. Investing in index funds means your money is spread out, which reduces risk. It's an easy way to invest because you don't have to pick individual stocks. They often have low fees and can be an excellent choice for long-term investors.

EXCHANGE-TRADED FUND (ETF)

An ETF is similar to an index fund but trades on the stock market like a regular stock. ETFs allow you to invest in various assets without buying each individually. They are flexible, usually have low fees, and can be purchased or sold anytime the market opens, making them a popular choice for new and experienced investors.

TARGET DATE FUNDS

Target date funds are designed to help you save for a specific retirement date, like 2035 or 2045. These funds automatically adjust their mix of stocks and bonds over time. When you're younger, they invest more aggressively in stocks for growth. As you get closer to retirement, they gradually shift to more stable investments like bonds. It's a "set it and forget it" approach, perfect for those who want a hands-off investment strategy.

PENSIONS

If you're fortunate enough to have a pension plan, it's a valuable asset for retirement. Pensions provide a guaranteed income stream for life based on your salary and years of service. These are becoming rarer in the private sector, but many public sector jobs still offer them. If you have a pension, it's essential to understand how it works, its benefits, and how it fits into your retirement strategy.

Now that we have addressed several different types of retirement contributions and investments, let's review some typical terminology that you might encounter.

RISK TOLERANCE

Risk tolerance is all about how comfortable you are with the ups and downs of investing. Think of it like a roller coaster: some people love the thrill and are okay with big drops (high-risk tolerance), while others prefer a smoother ride with fewer surprises (low-risk tolerance). Your risk tolerance helps you decide what investments are right for you. It's important to balance your comfort level with the potential rewards to stay calm and confident on your financial journey.

DIVERSIFICATION

Diversification is like having a variety of dishes at a potluck. Instead of putting all your eggs in one basket, you spread your money across different investments, like stocks, bonds, and real estate. This way, if one investment doesn't do well, the others might still perform okay, helping to balance things out.

Diversification helps reduce risk and gives you a better chance of reaching your financial goals by not relying on just one thing to succeed. Younger investors might choose a more aggressive strategy with a higher percentage of stocks. At the same time, those closer to retirement may prefer a more conservative approach with a greater emphasis on bonds and fixed-income investments.

Also, consider investment properties. As I mentioned earlier, we purchased two rental properties using cash from my husband's retirement. Now the properties help provide passive retirement income for us.

COMPOUND INTEREST

Compound interest is like a snowball rolling down a hill—it starts small but can grow big over time. When you invest or save money, you earn interest on your initial amount. With compound interest, you also earn interest on the interest you've already made. That means your money can grow faster the longer you keep it invested. It's one of the most powerful ways to build wealth, so the sooner you start saving or investing, the more time your money has to grow.

INSURANCE BASICS

Insurance is another critical component of financial planning. It protects against unexpected events and helps safeguard your assets. Let's explore some essential types of insurance you might consider.

Term life insurance. This type of insurance covers a specific period, typically 10, 20, or 30 years. If you pass away during the term, your beneficiaries receive a death benefit. Term life insurance is often the most affordable option and is ideal for covering specific financial obligations, like a mortgage or your children's education, during your working years. It's a straightforward way to provide financial security for your loved ones without breaking the bank.

Whole life insurance. Unlike term life insurance, whole life insurance covers your entire life and includes a savings component known as cash value. While it sounds appealing, whole life insurance is generally quite a bit more expensive than term life insurance and may not be the best option for everyone. The high premiums can limit your ability to invest in other areas, and the cash value growth is often slower than other investment opportunities. Many financial experts recommend buying term life insurance and investing the difference elsewhere for potentially higher returns.

Long-term care insurance. This type of insurance helps cover the costs of long-term care services not covered by regular health insurance or Medicare, such as nursing home care or in-home assistance. As we age, the likelihood of needing long-term care increases, and these costs can quickly deplete your savings. Long-term care insurance provides a safety net, ensuring access to necessary care without draining your retirement funds. It's essential to shop around and understand the coverage options, as policies can vary widely regarding benefits and costs.

Disability insurance. While not as commonly discussed, disability insurance is crucial for protecting your income in case you cannot work due to an illness or injury. There are two main types: short-term and long-term disability insurance. Short-term disability insurance covers a portion of your income for a limited period, usually three to six months, while long-term covers you for a longer duration, potentially until retirement. Ensuring you have adequate disability coverage can provide peace of mind and financial stability if you cannot work for an extended period.

COMBINING INSURANCE AND INVESTMENT STRATEGIES

When planning your financial future, it's essential to integrate insurance and investment strategies to create a comprehensive plan covering all bases. Here are some tips to help you combine these elements effectively.

EVALUATE YOUR NEEDS

Start by assessing your financial goals, risk tolerance, and any potential gaps in coverage. When deciding on the types and amounts of insurance you need, consider factors like your family situation, age, health, and income. These factors will help you tailor your insurance and investment strategies to fit your unique circumstances.

REVIEW AND ADJUST REGULARLY

Your financial situation and needs will evolve, so it's important to regularly review your insurance and investment strategies. Life events like marriage, the birth of a child, or a job change may require adjustments to your coverage or investment approach. Schedule annual check-ins to assess your progress and make any necessary updates.

SEEK PROFESSIONAL ADVICE

While it's important to educate yourself about insurance and investment options, seeking advice from a financial advisor can provide valuable insights tailored to your situation. An advisor can help you create a comprehensive financial plan, evaluate different investment and insurance products, and ensure you're on track to meet your long-term goals.

EDUCATE YOURSELF AND STAY INFORMED

The world of insurance and investments is constantly changing, with new products, regulations, and trends emerging regularly. Make it a habit to stay informed by reading financial news, attending workshops or webinars, and seeking resources to expand your knowledge. The more informed you are, the better equipped you'll be to make sound financial decisions.

Building a secure financial future involves a combination of thoughtful investment strategies and adequate insurance coverage. By understanding your options and making informed choices, you can create a solid foundation that supports your goals and provides peace of mind for you and your family. Whether you're just starting to plan for retirement or looking to optimize your insurance coverage, assessing your needs and exploring your options will pay off in the long run. With some planning and dedication, you can achieve financial stability and enjoy the journey along the way.

CREATE A CATCH-UP PLAN

Maximize contributions to retirement accounts, including catch-up contributions for those over age 50. In 2024, if you're older than 50, you can contribute $8,000 per year to an IRA. As I write this, there are 20 Mondays left in 2024.

That means you could invest $400 every Monday and hit that goal by the end of the year. That's a lot of money. I know. Even

$200 every Monday for the rest of the year, EVEN $100!!! If you were to start at the start of January 2025 investing $153.85 every week, you could max out those IRA contributions for the entire year.

Understanding the basics of insurance and investments doesn't have to be overwhelming. By exploring broad strategies and different options, you can confidently build a plan that secures your financial future. It's all about finding the right balance that fits your needs and goals to take on this next season.

18

YOUR SAFETY NET

NAVIGATING LIFE WITH JUST SOCIAL SECURITY

"There is a fountain of youth: it is your mind,
your talents, the creativity you bring to your life
and the lives of people you love."

Sophia Loren

What happens if you get to retirement age and find you have not been able to make enough money to invest in your golden years? All you have to live on is social security. You're definitely not alone. Many in our society were not able to prepare well for retirement and rely solely on Social Security payments. This includes my mother-in-law, Lorraine, who relies on social security only, along with an extra $65 a month she gets from her JCPenney pension.

To make this work, she lives in a lovely apartment, but in subsidized housing, so her rent payment is determined by a sliding scale based on her financial situation. She fills in the gaps through benefits such as, Heat and Electric Assistance Program (HEAP) and a little from the Supplemental Nutrition Assistance Program (SNAP) for groceries. We help her out wherever we can as well, but she finds a way to make this work.

Before she retired, Lorraine saved her money to visit Ireland and had a fantastic time. Her life regret is that she was too insecure to pursue her career of choice, but other than that, she's doing well.

Lorraine attended college late in life and graduated with her bachelor's degree at age 63. She did not pursue a degree for career advancement yet for her own self-fulfillment. She grew up in a home where educational encouragement (or any encouragement for that matter) was not an everyday practice. Could she have started a new chapter focused on a career in her chosen field and saved more for her retirement? She would likely say yes, but she doesn't regret the college journey.

The woman worked HARD, and we are all super proud of her.

Living on social security alone can be challenging, but it doesn't have to mean sacrificing happiness or a sense of purpose. Lorraine's story is a testament to the resilience, resourcefulness, and determination many midlife women embody. Through her journey, we can glean valuable lessons on navigating the challenges of living on a fixed income while still finding joy and fulfillment in everyday life.

BUILDING A STRONG SUPPORT NETWORK

One of the most crucial aspects of living on social security is recognizing and identifying the importance of community and support. Please reach out for help when you need it. One of the hardest things to do in life is to admit when you need help, and then to actually ask for it. Subsidized housing, government assistance programs like HEAP and SNAP, and local resources like senior meal programs can significantly ease the financial burden.

However, support isn't just about financial aid, yet also emotional and social support. Cultivate a network of friends, family, and community members who understand your situation and can offer companionship, advice, and a sense of belonging. Participate in community groups, senior centers, or volunteer organizations where you can give and receive support. Staying socially connected combats loneliness and opens doors to opportunities and resources you might not have known about. If it is not you, it very well could be a loved one, friend, or neighbor. We all need to look out for one another and jump in to help however we can.

PRIORITIZING HEALTH AND WELLNESS

Health is wealth, especially when living on a tight budget. Prioritize preventative care and healthy living to avoid costly medical bills down the road. Regular check-ups, staying active, and eating nutritious foods, even on a budget. Explore community gardens, farmer's markets, and local food co-ops for affordable, healthy options. Many areas also offer fitness programs designed for seniors, often at little to no cost.

Consider mindfulness practices like meditation or gentle yoga, which can help manage stress and improve mental health. These practices don't require expensive equipment and can be done at home, making them accessible no matter your financial situation.

EMBRACING MINIMALISM AND SIMPLIFYING LIFE

Living with less can be incredibly liberating. By simplifying your life, you can reduce financial stress and focus on what truly matters. Start by decluttering your home—sell or donate items you no longer need. Selling unwanted items brings in extra income and creates a more peaceful and organized living environment.

Downsizing to a smaller home or apartment also can be a smart move financially and emotionally. A smaller space is easier and cheaper to maintain, forcing you to be intentional about what you keep. Remember, a simpler life doesn't mean a lesser life— it means a life filled with purpose, where every item and every moment is cherished.

SMART FINANCIAL PLANNING

If you're approaching retirement age and still feel healthy and energetic, consider delaying your benefits. As mentioned earlier, each year you delay accepting Social Security, your monthly payment increases, providing additional financial security in the long run. During this time, you might explore part-time work or side hustles that align with your interests and skills. From consulting and freelance work to crafts and tutoring, there are many ways to generate income while maintaining flexibility.

Consult with a financial advisor or tax professional to understand the implications of additional income on your Social Security benefits. With careful planning, you can maximize your resources and avoid unnecessary penalties or reductions in benefits.

FINDING JOY IN THE SIMPLE THINGS

How do you continue to have an abundant life filled with joy if you aren't where you want to be, and money is tight? Living on a fixed income doesn't mean you give up on what brings you joy and pleasure. In fact, it can lead to a deeper appreciation for the simple things in life. Whether it's a walk in the park, visiting the local library, or sharing a homemade meal with loved ones, those moments can bring immense happiness.

Engage in low-cost yet fulfilling hobbies, such as reading, knitting, gardening, or painting. These activities provide a sense of purpose and achievement. If you've always wanted to learn something new, many community colleges and local organizations offer free or low-cost classes for seniors. Lifelong learning keeps the mind sharp and opens up new avenues for enjoyment.

VOLUNTEERING AND GIVING BACK

Even when money is tight, there's always something to give— your time, skills, and experience. Volunteering not only helps others but also enriches your own life. It provides structure, a sense of purpose, and the opportunity to connect with others. Depending on your experience, you could consider mentoring young people, volunteering at a local food bank, or participating in environmental projects, there are countless ways to make a difference. Any amount of time that you have to offer is always much appreciated.

Volunteering can also lead to new friendships, learning opportunities, and even potential job prospects. It's a way to stay active, engaged, and involved in your community while contributing to something bigger than yourself.

Living on social security alone requires careful planning, creativity, and resilience. By embracing a frugal, purposeful lifestyle, midlife women can find contentment and fulfillment even within financial constraints. Remember, it's not about how much money you have but how wisely you use it and how much joy you can create. With the right mindset and strategies, you can turn what may seem like a challenge into an opportunity for growth, connection, and happiness.

19

FRUGAL FOUNDATIONS

SMART CHOICES FOR THE LONG HAUL

"Money and success can't define us. True happiness comes from the inner fulfillment and simplicity of a well-lived life."

Arianna Huffington

You have made it this far in the book and have decided that you want the last season of your life to be AMAZING. You are ready to sacrifice now to rock it later. You are putting your financial goals first, or rather second to that of your family, and quitting this season of life is not an option.

Once deciding that this is who you are now, you no longer overspend and choose intentionality when you do spend. You value retirement and building a legacy over keeping up with the people next door, and you no longer care what others think about your financial decisions and how you choose to live your life.

I know I touched on this earlier but wanted to go over it again in a little more detail.

FRUGAL, THRIFTY, AND CHEAP

There are a few more things to consider when living a frugal life. Let's start with the word *frugal* and how it compares to *cheap* and *thrifty*.

Frugal does not mean *not* spending money. It means spending where you find value. Instead, I would ditch cable, luxury cars, purses, shoes, makeup, complicated skincare, and nails. I would much rather buy all the books I want to read and travel to every beach that calls my name, and that's all of them!

Cheap has a mean-spirited connotation. When someone is *cheap*, they put themselves first and to heck with anyone else, just to save a buck. People often use the terms thrifty and frugal interchangeably, but some key differences exist. While neither is a negative or a put-down, cheap can be demeaning.

Thrifty focuses on savings, while frugal focuses on value. Thrifty is about bargain hunting and finding the cheapest shoes, even if they are not the best quality. Frugal is finding the best quality shoes at the cheapest price, meaning through a sale, from a thrift store, or with a coupon.

You may face some challenges while adopting this lifestyle but stay strong.

SOCIAL PRESSURE AND LIFESTYLE EXPECTATIONS

I am a huge fan of Brené Brown. Her life philosophy aligns with mine and she is not shy about sharing her thoughts with whoever is willing to listen. It's no surprise that she's the author of several great books. One in particular that taught me a lot is *Daring Greatly*. In that book, she quotes Theodore Roosevelt, and the quote is a game changer for anyone worried about the opinions of others. I am so inspired by it that I want to print it out and hang it on the wall in my office. I use many different communication tools in my line of work, as with many these days, which include: a website, social media, and YouTube. These are fantastic modern tools to help grow a business, but it comes with a lot of vulnerability, you are a target and those who see your messages, will openly share their opinion and assume you and your audience will want to hear it. They express themselves loudly. It's the new order of today's world. Cancel culture is real and destructive.

If you want to lose faith in humanity, read the comment section of your posts or that of others!

The quote from Theodore Roosevelt is:

"It is not the critic who counts; not the man who points out how the strong man stumbles, or where the doer of deeds could have done them better. The credit belongs to the man who is actually in the arena, whose face is marred by dust and sweat and blood; who strives valiantly, who errs, who comes short again and again... who at the best knows in the end the triumph of high achievement, and who at the worst, if he fails, at least fails while daring greatly." *UGH...for me it pulls at those heartstrings every time. Does it impact you as well?*

If those who are sharing their opinions are not in the arena with you nor walking in your shoes, you do *not* need to listen to them. Do *not* allow that negativity to even enter your head space.

Through this book you may find some repeat information, but somethings are so important, I feel the need to say it one more time in a slightly different tone and probably using my teacher voice here and there, too.

A FEW THINGS TO REMEMBER

Resist the urge to keep up with social pressures to live in a certain type of house and drive a certain type of car. I'm not even sure I like those people I'm trying to impress. Dave Ramsey says in *The Total Money Makeover*, "We buy things we don't need with money we don't have to impress people we don't like." Find those who share your values, who like the same things you do, and who support you in your quest to live a frugal life.

HEALTHCARE COSTS AND UNEXPECTED EXPENSES

If you fall into the group that must pay for their own health insurance, brace yourself. Healthcare costs can break you. If you've retired and are too young for Medicare, the cost rests on your wallet.

Managing health care costs when it's not your area of expertise is confusing. We met with an insurance broker at no cost to us who helped us decide on the best options for our needs and budget. Because we are both pretty healthy and have an emergency fund capable of covering a lot of our deductible as needed, we were in a position to choose a less expensive health insurance with a lower monthly payment.

Consider supplemental insurance or health savings accounts (HSA) to bridge the gap and protect you from rising medical costs as you get older. Also, talk to your tax advisor as HSAs might be claimed as a tax write-off.

MARKET VOLATILITY AND ECONOMIC UNCERTAINTY

Market volatility and economic uncertainty can feel like a rollercoaster ride. One day you feel okay and the next the economy takes a sharp turn and sends you downhill with your stomach left behind. I encourage you to not spend too much time thinking about it and absolutely do not let it live in your head or your heart rent-free.

The majority of the time, these things do not affect our personal daily life. Although over time you might begin to notice more as we see the price of food increase, the cost of houses triple, and gas prices tip toe higher up so gradually, often you don't even see it coming.

But as a whole, we are fine.

I highly encourage you to seek the help of a professional advisor if you are looking at investments rise and fall. Don't panic. Talk to an expert. Do not try to navigate these waters if you don't have the knowledge to do so. The risk is too high.

EMBRACE RETIREMENT MINDSET

If you haven't gathered yet, I'm a total mindset nerd. I love all things positive and manifestation. I could write an entire book just on this topic alone!

Here are my thoughts:

Focus only on what you can control. Concentrate on areas of your money over which you have control. Aspects of your financial situation, such as budgeting, saving, and investing, are things in which you have the upper hand. You can't control the cost of Oreos, but you can control whether you buy Oreos or the store brand alternative.

Accept that some factors, such as market fluctuations, unexpected expenses, and the rising cost of living, will happen and are beyond your control. Instead, focus your energy on managing the variables within your reach. This is why an emergency fund is so important.

Practice gratitude for what you have and where you are. Focus on the abundance in your life rather than dwelling on scarcity. *Every. Single. Day.* Dr. Joe Dispenza writes in his book, *Becoming Supernatural: How Common People Are Doing the Uncommon,* "Something as simple as moving into an elevated state of joy, love, inspiration, or gratitude for five to 10 minutes a day can produce significant epigenetic changes in your health and body."

Appreciate the other aspects of retirement, not just the finances. No alarm clock, leisurely coffee, schedules that are out the window, and the ability to find new hobbies, learn the things you never had time to learn, as well as spending time with friends and family you never had enough time for when you were a full-time employee. Embrace flexibility and adaptability. Recognize that things may not happen the way you dreamed they would during retirement. However, being prepared for the unexpected and still finding the fun enthusiasm for which you've worked your entire life to get is part of the retirement journey. Find joy in everyday living.

Maintain flexibility and ride the waves not only with your money but with life in general. Be open to adjusting your financial goals, life choices, and spending habits as things shift.

Be a lifelong learner. This doesn't only mean educating yourself about finances unless you're a money geek (self admittedly). I have always wanted to learn to play the acoustic guitar. It's on my list and I even have a guitar. It was my dad's, and I kept it after he passed away. I am determined to make the time to learn.

I am also a HUGE lover of books, so learning by reading is my jam. I also learn a lot through watching interviews on YouTube from those who are experts in a specific field. My husband is not a book person, so he learns by watching videos. He still likes to learn new things, and now that he's retired as of 2022, he has more opportunities to do just that.

Prioritize holistic well-being, including physical health, emotional well-being, and social connections, as integral components of a fulfilling retirement. As I've shared, I'm on an overall personal health and wellness journey. This shouldn't stop just because you're getting older. On the contrary, there's no better time. I am also eyeball-deep in self-development. My bookshelves are full of great books just waiting for their turn to teach me something about being a better human.

Social connections get harder as we age and then somehow get easier again. We must really make an effort to reach out to our friends and make a date for coffee.

Hold on, that reminds me. I need to text Lisa and Rita right now for coffee soon. And Michelle, I haven't seen her in forever. Her daughter just left for college. We need to get together!

Invest your time in experiences that contribute to overall life happiness and that money isn't everything.

Choosing a frugal lifestyle means prioritizing your family's future and staying committed to your goals, no matter what. Once you embrace this mindset, intentional spending becomes second nature, and you find freedom in living true to your values. Remember, you're building something lasting—a secure retirement and a meaningful legacy—and that's worth far more than keeping up with anyone else. Stay the course, and trust in the choices you're making for the long haul.

20
THE FUN FACTOR

MAKING JOY A PRIORITY IN MIDLIFE

"True joy comes when you recognize that your life
is not just a gift to you, but to those around you."

Oprah

Now that we have covered just about everything that can
help save a little here and there, our electric bill decreased,
we have a solid emergency fund and have begun chipping away
at consumer debt using the snowball method or the avalanche
method (whatever you've chosen). Although all this is fantastic,
we find ourselves sliding off course often because our life feels
harder since we are not allowing ourselves to have as much freedom as we once did! All we do is talk about money and how to
increase our 401(k) contributions.

Where's all the fun? The book is called *Fundamentally Frugal* for
Peep Sake. (I know it's Pete's Sake, but since my youngest was

three, he called it *Peep* after the squishy Peeps from Easter, so now it no longer has anything to do with Pete.)

You can still have fun. There's a plethora of free things to do every season, but that also doesn't mean you can't go on a killer vacation. As I mentioned earlier, we are debt-free. We have a decent income coming in, and I still save all year for a February vacation on the Gulf Coast of Florida.

It's okay to save money from debt payoffs all year for a vacation in the dead of winter if that's what you choose. Consider a spending freeze a few times a year to be able to afford some fun in the sun, snow, or whatever tickles your fancy.

I mentioned in the beginning of the book that I implemented a 30-day, no-spend challenge, so I could go away for a few days to the lake to finish writing this book. It was sort of spontaneous because at home, with all the distractions (both good and not-so-good), I just could not finish this book. So, because it was not a significant planned expense, I cut back on other things to make it happen. Plus, I could use it as a tax write-off. A spending freeze or no-spend challenge is a great way to gather extra money for fun or a week-long getaway to the beach. It's also a smart way to store some money for the holidays.

There are frugal experts who believe that when you're on the debt freedom express train, every penny should go to debt. All vacations need to stop, and "you should not see the inside of a restaurant unless you're working there," according to Dave Ramsey.

Holi Cannoli, Batman! It took us a long time to get out of debt. This way sounds dreadful. I mean...I do not think weekly date nights are an answer, but maybe one date night each month and one food delivery each month would add some fun to your life.

While we were working on our debt payoff, we camped. My dad let us borrow his camper a few times, and then we ended up buying our own. We are still camping, and camping for us is pretty primitive—state campgrounds at $22 a night. There is no water, sewer, electricity, nor cable. Just the great outdoors and, if I can help it, a beautiful body of water.

Set up some boundaries and some limits, but please, don't stop having fun. Life is too short, and you never know what tomorrow will bring.

Living a frugal lifestyle and preparing for retirement doesn't mean you must sacrifice fun and entertainment. Finding creative and budget-friendly ways to enjoy life can be incredibly rewarding. By focusing on experiences rather than expenses, you can make lasting memories without breaking the bank. Let's explore some frugal activities for each season that can add joy to your life while keeping your finances in check.

I recognize that not all of my readers live where there are different seasons and winter is a "magical snowy wonderland" (insert sarcasm here). That makes me a little envious. At this season of life, I'm done with snow. If I could get my entire family to move to any of the sunshine states with me January through April, I would be out of here. Feel free to consider that if you don't get snow and ice skating is not an option because, well... there's no ice.

The same goes for cool fall days and leaf peeping (when you go for a walk or a ride with the sole intent of looking at the leaves changing colors at peak season). If you don't have the advantage of seeing the autumn colors in full bloom, consider saving your money for a trip to New England during peak season around late September or early October. It's truly stunning.

SPRING

Spring is a beautiful time to embrace the great outdoors and enjoy the fresh air and blossoming flowers. One frugal activity that's perfect for spring is visiting local parks and nature trails. Whether you're taking a leisurely walk, having a picnic, or simply enjoying the beauty of nature, spending time outside is a fantastic way to relax and recharge without spending a dime. Plus, many parks offer free or low-cost events like guided hikes or birdwatching tours that can enhance your experience.

Gardening is another excellent spring activity that's both frugal and fulfilling. You don't need a large plot of land to start; even a small container garden can bring joy and fresh produce to your table. Growing your herbs, vegetables, or flowers is a rewarding way to spend your time, and it can also save you money on groceries. If you're new to gardening, many communities offer free workshops or resources to help you get started.

Spring is also the perfect time for community festivals and farmers' markets. These events often feature live music, art exhibits, and local vendors selling handmade goods and fresh produce. Many of these festivals are free to attend and browsing the market stalls can be a delightful way to spend a sunny morning or afternoon. Supporting local businesses and farmers also is a great way to contribute to your community while enjoying yourself.

DIY craft projects are another fun and frugal way to enjoy the season. You can creatively repurpose items around your home into beautiful decorations or gifts. Whether you're making birdhouses, painting flowerpots, or creating handmade cards, crafting is a satisfying hobby that doesn't require a big budget. You can gather friends or family for a craft day and share supplies and ideas.

Lastly, consider spring cleaning and decluttering to have fun and feel productive. While cleaning might not sound like entertainment, refreshing your living space and eliminating clutter can be surprisingly satisfying. Turn on some music, open the windows, and make it a game to see how much you can accomplish in an afternoon. You can find items to sell or donate, which can bring in extra cash or benefit others in need.

SUMMER

Summer is the season for sunshine, adventure, and making the most of long, warm days. One frugal activity that's perfect for summer is exploring local swimming spots. Whether it's a nearby beach, lake, or community pool, cooling off in the water is a great way to beat the heat without spending much money. Pack a picnic, bring sunscreen, and enjoy a day of swimming and relaxation with friends or family.

Backyard barbecues are another classic summer activity that's both fun and budget friendly. Invite friends and neighbors for a potluck-style barbecue where everyone brings a dish to share. You can grill burgers or hot dogs and enjoy a laid-back afternoon of good food and great company. Plus, backyard games like frisbee, cornhole, or badminton can add to the fun without adding to the cost.

Summer is also an excellent time for outdoor movie nights. Set up a screen or a white sheet in your backyard, gather blankets and pillows, and enjoy a movie under the stars. You can stream a family favorite or a classic film and make popcorn or s'mores for a true movie theater experience. Outdoor movies are a fun way to spend quality time with loved ones and create lasting memories.

If you're looking for something active, consider hiking or bike riding. Exploring local trails and parks is a fantastic way to stay fit and appreciate the beauty of nature. Many trails are free to access, and biking is a cost-effective way to cover more ground and see new sights. Bring a camera to capture the scenery; you might even discover a new favorite spot in your area.

Finally, community events and free concerts are abundant in the summer months. Many towns and cities offer free outdoor concerts, festivals, and fairs that provide entertainment for all ages. Check out your local community calendar for upcoming events and enjoy the opportunity to experience live music, arts and crafts, and more without spending a fortune.

FALL

Fall is a magical time when the air turns crisp, and the leaves change color. It's the perfect season to enjoy cozy, frugal activities. One great fall activity is visiting a local pumpkin patch or apple orchard. Many orchards offer free entry, and you can spend the day picking apples or pumpkins, enjoying hayrides, and sipping on cider. It's fun to celebrate the season and bring home some fresh produce.

Leaf peeping is another frugal fall activity that can be relaxing and inspiring. Take a drive or a long walk through areas known for their beautiful fall foliage and enjoy the season's vibrant colors. Pack a thermos with hot cocoa or coffee and explore scenic byways or local parks to appreciate nature's beauty without spending a dime.

Fall is also the perfect time for DIY home decorating projects. Use natural elements like pinecones, acorns, and colorful leaves to create beautiful fall-themed decorations for your home. You can make wreaths, centerpieces, or garlands using items you find in your yard or on nature walks. Crafting with friends or family is a fun and frugal way to enter the season's spirit.

Baking and cooking are lovely fall activities that can fill your home with warmth and delicious aromas. Use seasonal produce like pumpkins, apples, and squash to make pies, soups, and other comforting dishes. Involve your family and enjoy a cozy day in the kitchen. Cooking at home is cost-effective and a great way to bond with loved ones.

Finally, consider attending local fall festivals or farmers' markets. Many communities host harvest festivals with live music, crafts, and seasonal foods. Admission is often free, and it's a fun way to enjoy the local culture and support small businesses. Whether sampling homemade treats or browsing artisan goods, fall festivals offer a delightful and affordable way to spend a day.

WINTER

Winter can be an enchanting time filled with cozy, frugal activities that warm the heart. One great winter activity is visiting local holiday light displays. Many communities put on free or low-cost light shows during the holiday season, which can be fun and festive to get into the spirit of the season. Bundle up, bring a thermos of hot cocoa, and enjoy a stroll or drive through twinkling winter wonderlands.

Ice skating is another classic winter activity that's both fun and affordable. Many towns have outdoor skating rinks that offer free or low-cost admission. Whether you're a seasoned skater or a beginner, gliding on the ice is a joyful way to embrace the winter season. Plus, it's great exercise that feels like something other than a workout. Winter is also an excellent time for home movie marathons. Cozy up with blankets and pillows, make some popcorn, and enjoy a day of watching your favorite films. You can choose a theme or a series and involve the whole family in the fun. Streaming services and libraries offer plenty of entertainment options without leaving home. If your kids are older, it's always fun to dust off old family videos to peruse, especially if they have friends and/or significant others visiting! Just don't pull out the wedding video, if you have one. The old saying is that it's a surefire way to tell your guests that it's time to go home. *Of course, if that's your intent, then go ahead, dust it off, and play it for your guests!*

Consider making homemade gifts and decorations if you're looking for something crafty. Winter is the perfect time to get creative and make personalized gifts for friends and family. From knitted scarves to handmade ornaments, crafting can be a fulfilling and frugal way to spread joy during the holiday season. You can also gather with friends for a craft day and share supplies and ideas.

Finally, embrace the season by playing in the snow—that is if you live in an area where it actually snows! These days, who knows where it snows! Whether building a snowman, having a snowball fight, or sledding down a nearby hill, playing in the snow is a timeless and free way to enjoy winter. Bundle up and let your inner child out to play, and you'll find that the simplest activities can bring the most joy.

Living a frugal lifestyle doesn't mean giving up on fun and entertainment. Embracing frugal activities can enhance your life by focusing on experiences that bring joy and create lasting memories. By exploring these budget-friendly activities throughout the year, you can enjoy each season to its fullest without breaking the bank. Whether crafting, exploring nature, or spending time with loved ones, there are countless ways to have fun while living frugally. Remember, it's not about how much you spend but the memories you make and the joy you share with others. So go ahead, have fun, and enjoy the journey to a frugal and fulfilling life!

21

CONCLUSION

"Laugh, Love, and Save: Joy on a Budget."

Sara Conklin

As I completed this book and was sitting in my office reviewing it one more time, I wondered what additional information I could add. I pictured myself thinking about 14 things I should have included to help you with your goals and your money AFTER the book has been published. If that's the case, then I will publish a follow-up for you!

This was a brutal, yet beautiful project to work on for me. The first chapter was a DOOZY and gosh, I needed to give myself some grace on feeling all the feels in getting it completed.

My true hope for you is:

I hope that you make it through just a few more years of work if you are still struggling with debt so that you can live the rest of your life without that weight on your shoulders.

I hope that you don't think it's too late to do great things. You have so many amazing years ahead of you to make all your dreams come true.

I hope that you give to others daily. Remember, we are all here to serve each other and give the smallest gesture of kindness, smiling at someone and holding the door, it matters. Every *little* bit of kindness made a very *big* difference in the world.

I hope that you choose gratitude over bitterness, anger, and complaints. You cannot be fearful and grateful at the same time.

I hope you make the rest of your time on this earth wonderful. Strive to have no regrets once your time here is done. Love with all your heart and tell the people that.

I hope you realize that money is not everything and cannot fill all the needs of us humans.

Finally, I hope you have lots of fun! Enjoy the journey, run like Phoebe from *Friends,* dance like Elaine from *Seinfeld, laugh* like the iconic Robin Williams, may he rest in peace. Do things that make your heart happy and don't forget to save up for the special ones.

I'd love to continue to motivate you to live your best life! Stay *Fundamentally Frugal!*

Let's stay connected!

youtube.com/@saraconklinfrozenpennies
facebook.com/frozenpenniesblog
frozenpennies.com

ABOUT THE AUTHOR

Sara is a multifaceted individual, both personally and professionally. She is a wife, mother, grammy, and the creative force behind the Frozen Pennies website, and thriving YouTube channel. With a degree in English and experience as a former teacher, Sara's journey led her to become a Certified Financial Coach through Ramsey Solutions. Drawing from her rich lineage of strong, frugal, and independent women, she has mastered the art of living frugally while cherishing life's simple pleasures, whether it's losing herself in a good book, soaking up the sun at the beach, or cherishing moments with loved ones.

Her motivation to pen this book stems from personal experience. Having grappled with the suffocating weight of consumer debt while juggling responsibilities such as caring for aging parents, guiding children through the maze of college decisions, and planning for retirement, Sara intimately understands the challenges of midlife finances.

Unlike other books on frugality, Sara's work uniquely focuses on navigating this pivotal life stage, demonstrating how one can prepare for the future while embracing a more financially responsible and frugal lifestyle. Through her insightful guidance, readers will discover that achieving debt freedom, mastering budgeting, and embracing frugality are not only attainable but also enriching experiences that pave the way for a fulfilling life.